COUNTERFEIT CHARISMA

THE AGE OF FALSE PROPHETS

BY

DENNIS JAMES WOODS

LIFE TO LEGACY

Counterfeit Charisma
The Age of False Prophets

by Dennis James Woods, Copyright ©2018

ISBN-13: 978-1-947288-39-3
ISBN-10: 1-947288-39-3

Printed in the United States
10 9 8 7 6 5 4 3 2 1

Cover design by: Legacy Design Inc
Legacydesigninc@gmail.com

Published by
Life To Legacy, LLC
P.O. 1239
Matteson, IL 60443
877-267-7477
www.Life2Legacy.com
Life2legacybooks@att.net

TABLE OF CONTENTS

"Beware of the false prophets, who come to you in sheep's clothing, but inwardly are ravenous wolves. "You will know them by their fruits. "A good tree cannot produce bad fruit, nor can a bad tree produce good fruit. "Every tree that does not bear good fruit is cut down and thrown into the fire. "So then, you will know them by their fruits."
Matthew 7:15-16, 18-20 NASB

A HEARTBREAKING STORY

Some years ago, a heartbreaking story made the evening news in Chicago, regarding an obscure pastor of a small church that perpetrated a deliberate deception that affected his entire congregation. This minister persuaded his parishioners that the end of the world was coming an would occur on a particular date. As this ominous day edged closer, his teaching became more emphatic insisting that everyone needed to prepare for the coming of the Lord. The pastor encouraged that congregates tell their friends and loved ones about the coming apocalypse, but invariably they were all turned down. Despite all of the naysayers, the pastor and his parishioners could not be deterred no matter how others criticized or disbelieved.

Over the course of a few weeks, the pastor started teaching on how his members should start preparing for the end of the world. He encouraged people to clear out their bank accounts and bring the money to the church. Those with jobs, he encouraged to quit because employment and careers would no longer be necessary. Being faithful to what his pastor was teaching, a man who was a husband and father of five, gainfully employed for years on a good municipal job, without warning, walked into his boss's office and summarily quit.

On the day that was supposed to be the end, all the faithful members gathered at the church where they all worshiped and prayed, waiting for the Lord to return. Hour after hour, they tarried and hoped. As the minutes and hours ticked by, inevitably the clock struck twelve midnight. It was at that defining moment that it became dreadfully clear that they had all been deceived.

This tragic story is disturbing on many levels, the chief one being they were all deceived by a false prophet. One could ask, Why didn't his members simply read the Bible for themselves, because it clearly teaches that no man knows the day or the hour of the Lord's return. This question points to a greater reality when discussing the amount of influence a false prophet can have over people. In the ears of the hearers, the false prophet's word is just as, and in many cases, even more, authoritative than the Scriptures themselves. Yes, those deceived by a false prophet can be blamed for their part, but that is not at all mitigating for the culpability that a false prophet bears. False prophets are vessels that Satan uses to kill, steal and destroy. While promising wealth, prosperity and ease of life, their words lead to confusion, dissolution, depression and ultimately destruction.

Unfortunately, this story is not at all unusual. There are thousands of instances like this one that takes place all over the United States and throughout the world every day. There are endless stories of dysfunctional abusive churches headed up by evil and egotistical ministers only out to enrich and make a name for themselves. Many of these stories are more tragic than the one we mentioned here. Some of the more heinous cases lead to mental breakdown and even death. People are making life changing decisions based upon the word from a false prophet who does not have the people's welfare in mind.

As in the case of the husband who walked away from his job, he did go back to his employer and begged for his job back, but to no avail. However, this unfortunate story is not just about him but it's also about his family; his wife and kids who have to live with the embarrassment and disruption the man's bad decision caused. But by far, the worst thing that can happen to anybody that follows or believes a false prophet is that they could end up falling away from the faith, lost and destined to eternal damnation. The latter is what makes this phenomenon such a critical issue. Of the many signs of the end-times that Jesus warned would come on this world, the coming of many false prophets is one of them. As we find ourselves in the midst of the last days, the age of the false prophet is among us.

COUNTERFEIT CHARISMA

THE AGE OF FALSE PROPHETS

INTRODUCTION

The first edition of *Counterfeit Charisma* was written in 2001, to shed light on the increasing infiltration of counterfeit charismatic gifts operating in churches throughout the United States and many parts of the world. The premise of the first book was based upon a solemn warning at the end of *the Sermon on the Mount*, where the Lord tells us about what false prophets would claim on Judgment Day. In Matthew 7:21-23, the Lord warns that there would be those that stand before Him and declare: "Lord, Lord, did we not prophesy in your name and in your name drive out demons and in your name perform many miracles?' Then I will tell them plainly, 'I never knew you. Away from me, you evildoers.'"

Each time I read this passage, I cannot help but reflect on the great implications and significance that the Lord's words carry here, especially now that we are in the 21st century, where there are so many who operate in one or more of these three gifts. The text is explicit and leaves little room for doubt as to the gravity of what the Lord is declaring. Astonishingly, there would be many people who believed themselves to be Christians, who thought they were operating under the anointing of the Holy Spirit, who prophesied, cast out devils, and performed miracles, but had no saving relationship with Jesus. One can only imagine the trauma of that situation where these individuals attempt to convince a sagacious, all-knowing God of their legitimacy based on their claim to have operated in some charismatic gift.

If I were to paraphrase what their defense may be, they would in essence be saying, "Lord if we were not legitimate Christians, how else could we have prophesied, cast out demons, and performed miracles in your name?" Yes, indeed that is the critical question that is now before us. How could they have done these powerful works, and yet Christ not know them?

It is interesting that the Lord does not argue with them about whether they did or did not actually do what they claimed to have done, because that's not the real issue at hand. Rather, the Lord goes right to the core of the issue, which is not the works they claim to have done, but the relationship between Himself and them. It is that precise point with which we should all be concerned. At the end of the day, it is not about the prophecy or the miracles, but it is about what work the Lord has done in your heart. Does the Lord know you? As it pertains to the *many* spoken of in this text, a redeeming relationship with Christ had never occurred. They were living and operating under deception, not salvation.

Of the many fascinating aspects about this passage, one that is worth taking note of is that there were three charismatic gifts or enablements identified specifically in verse 22, which are: *prophecy, casting out devils*, and *performing miracles*. Since the context of this passage is Judgment Day, which is yet future, these individuals had to have operated during the era where works are done in the name of Jesus, which began at Pentecost and is ongoing today. This is the Church age. Since the individuals that Jesus identifies in this passage must exist during the Church age, some critical questions must be asked. What Christians operate in these gifts? In what churches, denominations, or organizations are these gifts commonly found? I emphasize "commonly" because the Bible declares that there would be "many," which indicates that their operation and use are widespread. Equally intriguing is the fact that these individuals believed themselves to be legitimate Christians who undoubtedly performed their works among the Christian or Church communities.

One of the great mysteries of the kingdom is the existence of impostors that infiltrate the ranks of God's people. Tares grow together among the wheat, meaning that not everyone who claims to be a Christian is one. In verses 21-23, we see individuals on Judgment Day using their gifts as a basis to defend their legitimacy to no avail. However, in verses 15-16, Jesus warns, "Beware of false prophets, who come to you in sheep's clothing, but inwardly they are ravenous wolves. You will know them by their fruits…." So, not everyone who looks like a Christian or even claims to be a Christian, no matter what their status or title, is a Christian.

SIGNS OF THE END TIMES

During the Mount Olivet discourse, Jesus' disciples ask the following questions, "What are the signs of His coming and the end of the world?" Christ responds with a list of prophetic signs that will characterize the time just prior to His return at the end of the age, such as: wars and rumors of wars, nation rising against nation, kingdom against kingdom, famines, earthquakes, and pestilences (Matt. 24:4-8). However, another sign, just as important as the others, is found in verse 11, where the text reads,"…and many false prophets will appear and deceive many people." It is at this decisive point where this book's emphasis will be. In this book, *Counterfeit Charisma, The Age of False Prophets*, I focus intensely upon the prevalence of false prophets and false prophecy operating in numerous churches, and how many people are being deceived on a daily basis.

Since Pentecostals and Charismatics are the sectors of Christianity that rely heavily on the "movement" of the Holy Spirit, where prophecy, deliverance (casting out demonic spirits), and miraculous healing typically occur during deliverance services, or at least are claimed to be occurring, then it is of the utmost importance that these same churches, organizations, and individuals be extra vigilant in assuring that they are not hosting counterfeits. In general, other denominations (i.e., Evangelicals, Baptists, Methodists, Presbyterians, and several other non-Pentecostal/Charismatic denominations) are not as vulnerable to this phenomenon, because operating in the "sign gifts" in the church is not a part of their doctrine or practice. However, this does not mean they are immune to this phenomenon, or that they do not have significant problems in other areas, but from the standpoint of the gifts named in the text, they are less apt to be affected by false prophets that operate in these gifts. However, false doctrine and deception can affect anyone, regardless of denominational affiliation or geographic location.

In the midst of a growing Charismatic and Pentecostal movement throughout the world, care and caution must be taken by these groups to guard against intrusions of counterfeit gifts operating in their organizations and churches. An unhealthy attraction for spiritual things such as "signs and wonders" can lead to an unbalanced desire for anything labeled as *supernatural*. Jesus admonishes the Pharisees for the very same thing when He says: "A wicked and adulterous generation seeks after a sign…"(Matt. 16:4).

Therefore, the purpose of this book is not to convert the false prophets, because they are ambassadors of the kingdom of darkness. They have their reward. However, the purpose of this book is to warn those who could be deceived by false prophets and have their lives and even their relationship with God ruined. False prophets are out for themselves and are liars who use Jesus' name as a cover to feed upon the sheep.

WHAT THIS BOOK IS NOT

Though I will be examining at length the operation of false prophets in the Church, it is equally important to distinguish what this book is not. This *is not* a study where I expose or name supposed false prophets. There are numerous books and programs on the bookshelves and on the airwaves these days that name individuals and label them as false. It is not my calling or purpose in writing this book to do that. God already knows who the false prophets are. Secondly, this book is not to promote the doctrine of the *cessationist*. In the theological sense, a cessationist is an individual who believes that the spiritual gifts, found in 1

Corinthians chapters 12 and 13, have ceased. Those who espouse this doctrine purport that the gifts are no longer operating in the church at all. The following passage is one of the texts used to back this doctrine:

> Charity never faileth: but whether there be prophecies, they shall fail; whether there be tongues, they shall cease; whether there be knowledge, it shall vanish away. For we know in part, and we prophesy in part. But when that which is perfect is come, then that which is in part shall be done away.
>
> 1 Corinthians 13:8-10

To the cessationist, the reference to *prophecy failing* and *tongues ceasing* is a prediction of the end of the operation of these gifts. Also, to the cessationist, the reference to the coming of that which is perfect speaks of the closing of the *canon*[1] (a Greek word meaning "measuring stick") of Scripture, which occurred in 397 A.D. at Carthage, where the list of the books of the Bible was finalized.[2] Since the canon of the Scripture was closed, the cessationist believes that God is no longer giving any *new revelation*, via tongues, prophecies, or by any other means. The cessationist also believes that the working of miracles also went out with the age of the apostles.

Again, the cessationist's view *is not* the position I take in this book. I believe that the gifts are still in operation. However, I do not believe that all the spiritual gifts we see in many churches are always authentic manifestations.

Let me be clear, though I'm not a cessationist, I'm not a *sensationalist* either! I'm not in support of all the elaborate, flamboyant antics and fads which defy church order and sound doctrine. I'm skeptical of many of the contemporary doctrinal trends that run rampant through many churches. In my opinion, all practices not clearly backed by Scripture and sound doctrine are questionable. If a practice doesn't align with sound doctrine, it should be avoided altogether. At the end of the day, if it's not in line with the Word, it's in lockstep with the world. The Scriptures are explicit:"For all that is in the world, the lust of the flesh, and the lust of the eyes, and the pride of life, is not of the Father, but is of the world. And the world passeth away, and the lust thereof: but he that doeth the will of God abideth for ever" (1 John 2:16-17, KJV).

ARE THERE STILL PROPHETS TODAY?

Are there still prophets today is a very controversial question. To that I would answer both *yes* and *no*. Yes, if you consider that there is a New Testament gift and office of the prophet. Though some draw a strict line between the functioning of the *office* of the prophet and the *gift* of prophecy, this point will not be labored in this book. The office of the prophet is found in 1 Corinthians 12:28 and Ephesians 4:11, and is directly related to the functioning of prophets in the church. There are other references to prophets as being part of the foundation that has already been laid (Eph. 2:20). On this basis, you have difficulty arguing that prophets *cannot* exist today, because they are said to be in the Body of Christ, and they do have a role to play in the local church (1 Cor. 14:29). Now, how many will there be, are they to function in every church, are they itinerant, how often do rise (once a generation, once a century etc.) and to whom are they ministering, to the universal church, a nation, or just a local phenomenon, are just a few difficult questions. On the other hand, we must acknowledge that the cessationist would assert that there are none today that fulfill that office or gift based on the reasons stated previously.

No, prophets do not exist today if you mean do they operate the same way that they did in the Old Testament; here is the reason why. Jesus Christ, who is the central theme and fulfillment of prophetic revelation, being the very Word of God manifested in the flesh, has already come, died, and resurrected. With His first advent being fulfilled, that changed the focus of prophetic revelation, which in the Old Testament anticipated and prophesied about His coming and atoning sacrifice for the sin of the world. Therefore, most Old Testament prophecy was woven throughout history into a prophetic tapestry to reveal Christ. Jesus spoke directly to this issue when he was instructing His disciples after His resurrection:

> Then He said to them, "These are the words which I spoke to you while I was still with you, that all things must be fulfilled which were written in the Law of Moses and the Prophets and the Psalms concerning Me." And He opened their understanding, that they might comprehend the Scriptures.
>
> Luke 24:44-45, NKJV

A famous statement by St. Augustine says *"the new is in the old concealed, and the old is in the new revealed."* Now that the focus of Old Testament prophecy has been revealed in Christ, the New Testament focus of prophecy has changed to what Christ is saying primarily to the Church and about the coming of His kingdom in full manifestation, which anticipates His Second coming, the culminating prophetic event of this age and ages to come. Christ is therefore the central focus and foundation of prophetic revelation in the New Testament. As declared in the book of Revelation, "the testimony of Jesus, is the spirit of prophecy" (Rev. 19:10).

The epistle to the Hebrews opens with these words that set the stage for the right frame of reference in which prophetic revelation in this dispensation should be understood. "In the past God spoke to our ancestors through the prophets at many times and in various ways, but in these last days he has spoken to us by his Son, whom he appointed heir of all things, and through whom also he made the universe."(Hebrews 1:1-3). Clearly, God has made a distinction in the function of the central role of the prophet. In the Old Testament, he chose to speak through prophets, but today in the New Testament He speaks to us through Jesus Christ.

During the age of the Church, Christ through the Holy Spirit dwells within us and through His indwelling relationship leads and guides us in all truth (Col. 1:27, John 16:13). Due to the direct relationship that we have with Christ, and because we can hear His voice (John 10:27), a prophet as such is not essential, because God now speaks to us through Christ, and Christ speaks to us through the Spirit and His Word.

In the Old Testament, prior to Christ, all they had was the prophet that prophesied what thus sayeth the Lord to the people, nations, and kings. However, the role of prophets today is more auxiliary and supportive, for the edification of the body, to help bring the saints to maturity and unity of the faith (Eph. 4:11-13). Therefore, to all the prophets of today, let them declare what Christ is saying to the church. Our personal agendas mean nothing, and prophesying for entertainment purposes is foolish and meaningless. Let God be true and every man a liar. The apostle Peter admonishes us:

> If anyone speaks, *let him speak* as the oracles of God. If anyone ministers, *let him do it* as with the ability which God supplies, that in all things God may be glorified through Jesus Christ, to whom belong the glory and the dominion forever and ever. Amen.
>
> 1 Peter 4:11, NKJV

My study of the role of the prophet in the church will be continued in the following chapter.

CHAPTER ONE

THE TRUE PROPHET

Before we can get an understanding of what is a false prophet, we must first examine the office and operation of a true prophet. Therefore, the following shall be a cursory examination of the office of a prophet, but by no means is an exhaustive study of the same. Since the focus of this book is false prophets, the summary of true prophets shall be basic.

One of the first things that we must understand about the prophetic office is that a true prophet must be *called by God*. You cannot go to school to learn to be a prophet like you can to be a medical doctor or a lawyer, though there are some that advocate for the concept of "the schools of prophets" (more on this later). The necessity of calling negates any self-appointed individuals who *call themselves* to the office of the prophet or who are merely installed into that office by men. God's calling is necessary, because it is God who determines whom He will speak through. A human being cannot make that determination. Both the prophet and priest served in mediatory capacities. Whereas the priest served in the temple and sanctuary offering up sacrifices and prayers, and performing a number of liturgical duties to God on behalf of the people, the prophet, on the other hand, spoke to the people on behalf of God.

> *If the prophet declared to speak for the Lord, his prophecy had to come to past, one-hundred percent of the time, because he declared "thus saith the Lord."*

Prophets acted as a mouthpiece for God and received their prophecies directly from Him to reveal whatever purpose or plan God had determined to disclose. God directed the prophet to give messages to individuals, nations and kings to reveal His purposes, plans and righteousness in order to bring conformity to His will. The prophet spoke to God's people from His divine perspective, which is holy, omnipresent, omniscient, and omnipotent. This point cannot be overstated. The fact that God's ways are not men's ways often meant that God's people were not aligning with His will, and thus the prophets' role was to say "thus saith the Lord," which was in stark contrast to "what sayeth the people" who were often in rebellion against God.

Since God is one, a true prophet could only speak for the one true God. Prophets were also preachers, as evidenced in Jonah 3:2: "Arise, go unto Nineveh, that great city, and preach unto it the preaching that I bid thee (Jonah 3:2, KJV). Though prophets were God's mouthpiece, they were not given license to alter God's message (Deut. 4:2, 18:18).

In the Old Testament, prophets could also be identified by two other designations, which were *Man of God*, or *Seer*. Prophets were normally men, but there were also women as well, prophetesses, who were called and anointed of God to perform their ministry. Prophets could receive their messages by external or internal voice and by visions and dreams. Since the prophet was the mouthpiece for God, the prophet's message was often prefaced by the phrase, *Thus saith the Lord* (KJV) or *This is what the Lord says* (NIV), or another preface of a similar nature.

A true prophet must speak in the name of the Lord. A true prophet may produce a sign or a wonder, but the vast majority of prophets were not endowed with miraculous faculties. A true prophet could have predictions fulfilled visibly. A true prophet's message would agree with all of the previous prophetic revelations. True prophets of God wrote by the inspiration of the Holy Spirit, and were held to the highest standards of moral character and conduct.

Old Testament prophets fall into two basic categories, either literary or nonliterary prophets. Prophets were also distinguished by the terms *major* and *minor* prophets. These designations speak to the volume of the writing, but not the sense of importance. Since all Scriptures were given by inspiration of God, then no prophet is more inspired than any other one.

Under the Law, the prophet was characterized by messages of national rebuke, as Israel or Judah were in moral decline and unfaithful to God. These prophets also served as God's spokesmen in revealing God's prophetic plan for the ages, such as found in Isaiah, Daniel, Ezekiel, and others. Old Testament prophets continued until Malachi.

According to the Protestant tradition, there were no prophets for four-hundred years after Malachi. This four-hundred year gap was called the *Intertestamental Period,* the period that encompasses the close of the Hebrew bible and the beginning of the Christian New Testament. On the other hand, the Catholic tradition would disagree with that assertion, as they would claim other prophets that are found in the *Apocrypha*, which is part of the Catholic Bible, but not in the Protestant Bible, which ends with Malachi. In the Protestant tradition, the books of the Apocrypha did not meet the criteria for inspiration and agreement with other prophetic revelations found in the Old Testament. Therefore, they were not included in the canon of Scriptures making up the current sixty-six books of the Bible.

> *Prophets had the formidable task of delivering a word from the Lord that in many cases, was particularly unfavorable to stiff-necked people. Prophets were often shunned, rejected and even killed.*

The first New Testament prophet was John the Baptist, who was prophesied to come in Isaiah 40:3, "The voice of him that crieth in the wilderness, Prepare ye the way of the LORD...." Though John ministered during New Testament times, as to dispensation, they were still under the Law. It is of John the Baptist that Jesus declared, "I tell you, among those born of women there is no one greater than John..." (Matt. 11:11). It is of John the Baptist that Jesus said the following, "For all the Prophets and the Law prophesied until John. And if you are willing to accept it, he is the Elijah who was to come" (Matt.11:13-15; also see Mal. 4:5).

THE PROPHETIC MISSION

In the book of Jeremiah, the prophetic mission is described. The passage reads: "See, I have this day set thee over the nations and over the kingdoms, to root out, and to pull down, and to destroy, and to throw down, to build, and to plant"(Jer.1:10). According to this passage, prophets had great responsibility and were revered by the people. Since the prophet had great influence, God had a very practical test to prove whether they were the Lord's prophet or not. If the prophet declared to speak for the Lord, his prophecy had to come to pass, without error, one-hundred percent of the time, because he prefaced his prophecy with the declaration "thus saith the Lord."

In Deuteronomy 18, the Lord instructs Israel about the prophet:

> But the prophet who presumes to speak a word in my
> name that I have not commanded him to speak, or who

speaks in the name of other gods, that same prophet shall die.'And if you say in your heart, 'How may we know the word that the LORD has not spoken?'—when a prophet speaks in the name of the LORD, if the word does not come to pass or come true, that is a word that the LORD has not spoken; the prophet has spoken it presumptuously. You need not be afraid of him.

Deuteronomy 18:20-22, ESV

As we can see from this passage, there was no room for error when it came to the prophet's prophecy. However, at this point an important distinction has to be made. If a prophet is speaking *"in the name of the Lord,"* this means God has given him a *direct message*, and the prophet must give it to the people exactly as the Lord has said. Under those circumstances, the prophecy has to be one hundred percent accurate because it came directly from God, and He cannot make a mistake. This is why verse 22 states, "if the word does not come to pass or come true, that is a word that the LORD has not spoken; the prophet has spoken it presumptuously," meaning that the prophet has *supposed* this is what the Lord said, or would say, or they have straight-out lied about the Lord saying something that He did not say at all.

CAN A TRUE PROPHET GET IT WRONG?

It should be understood that though the prophet can receive a message from the infallible God, the prophet himself is fallible and subject to error. Though mouthpieces for God, prophets are not automatons devoid of life, emotions, and personality who receive messages from God 24/7, but are fallen, sinful human beings that make mistakes. Harsh critics that claim there are no prophets today often apply the one-hundred-percent-accuracy rule to prove prophetic legitimacy. However, a true prophet speaking from *his heart* can be wrong by speaking emotionally, optimistically, or according to his own understanding. Such prophecies can prove to be wrong, but do not necessarily negate legitimacy. An example of this can be found in the Scriptures:

After David was settled in his palace, he said to Nathan the prophet, "Here I am, living in a house of cedar, while the ark of the covenant of the LORD is under a tent." Nathan replied to David, "Whatever you have in mind, do it, for God is with you." But that night the word of God came to Nathan, saying: "Go and tell my servant David, 'This is what the LORD says: You are not the one to build me a house to dwell in.'"

1 Chronicles 17:1-4

Here Nathan capitulates to his king's known desire to build the Lord's temple (1 Chron. 28:2). Nathan *incorrectly* tells David, "Whatever you have in mind, do it, for God is with you." This was not the case! God *did not* tell Nathan to say that to David. God *was not* going to do whatever David had in mind concerning his desire to build the Lord a temple. That very night the Lord corrected Nathan—and notice the big distinction in the message this time: "Go and tell my servant David, '*This is what the LORD says...*,'" not this is what *Nathan* says.

What can we learn from this? Just because Nathan is God's prophet does not mean *everything* Nathan says comes from God, because God is not inspiring prophetic messages to the prophet every hour of the day. Only whatever "Thus saith the Lord" is what comes from God. The rest is on the prophet. "Thus saith the Lord" means what's following is what the Lord has spoken directly word for word. The question is, should Nathan be declared a false prophet over this mistake? No, because Nathan, like all people, makes mistakes. And the fact that the Lord does speak to Nathan to give a corrected word proves that Nathan did hear from God. Being corrected doesn't diminish his credibility. The indictment against false prophets is that God *didn't send them, but they prophesied anyway*. Though Nathan did make a mistake, he was still called and sent by God.

Prophets have an awesome responsibility to take care in what they say to the people. People will automatically assume that everything the prophet says is from God. The problem with prophets speaking a word from their own heart is that it can cause harm and confusion. Therefore, it is the prophet's responsibility to be clear when they are speaking from their own opinion. In 1 Cor. 7:12, the apostle Paul makes a similar distinction when giving instruction concerning marriage. He says, "To the rest I say this (I, not the Lord)." This should not be taken as Paul's take-it-or-leave-it opinion,[3] because Paul did have apostolic authority to build up the church (2 Cor. 13:10), which gave him some latitude to speak in cases where Jesus did not give direct or specific instructions.

NEW TESTAMENT PROPHETS

With the close of the Old Testament, the age of the Old Testament prophets as such also came to a close. Although the Old Testament closed with the book of Malachi and New Testament began with the Gospel narratives, the times covered by the Gospels were still under the Dispensation of Law, or the Old Covenant. According to Jesus, much of Old Testament prophecy was concerning Him (Luke 24:44). However, with the first advent of the Lord and redemption accomplished, New Testament prophecy took on a new character and emphasis. Unlike the prophets of old who were sent by God to a whole nation like Israel and Judah, New Testament prophecy was now focused on the development of the church. For the most part, the prophet's office has given way to offices in the Church. Therefore, during New Testament times, prophets were less conspicuous than their Old Testament counterparts. In the last few decades, though, there has been a surge of ministers carrying the title apostle and prophet, the vast majority of churches are headed by individuals that carry the title pastor.

During the Church age, the New Testament prophet's ministry is characterized as being one of the five-fold ministry *Gifts* given to the church, for the perfecting of the saints and the work of the ministry (Eph. 4:8-13). Additionally, the New Testament prophets' role was different from their Old Testament predecessors. Although New Testament prophets could have predictive unctions, primarily they went forth in the ministry of *forth telling*, as opposed to the predictive *foretelling*. Forth telling, or preaching, was primarily for the comfort, edification, and exhortation of the church (1 Cor.14:3). However, New Testament prophets are gifted to understand all mysteries and all knowledge (1 Cor. 13:2), and of having the discernment to reveal the secrets of men's hearts (1 Cor. 14:25).

Though the New Testament prophets added no new revelation to the canon of the Scriptures, they were given wisdom in the mysteries pertaining to the church hidden from the prophets of old (Eph. 3:5). Though some make a sharp distinction between the *gift* of prophecy and the *office* of the prophet, not all expositors see a clear line of demarcation between the two, particularly since the New Testament Church typically functions under either an Episcopal (Greek—*episkopos*)[4] bishops or Presbyterian (Greek—*presbyteros*)[5] elders structure. However, these two structures are not exclusive, because many churches have congregational structures or are autocratic, where the pastor alone leads the church. Some pastors even carry the title apostle and/or prophet.

Since prophets are those individuals who are the mouthpieces for God declaring His Word, by the broadest sense of that definition, any of the five-fold ministries and/or the laity can function prophetically. Declaring what saith the Lord, from the Scriptures, in the simplest sense meets the definition of *forth telling*. God can unction any believer to speak prophetically, but by doing so does not automatically make them "a prophet."

For example, in the early 2000s, around '04 or '05, I preached at a faith-based women's shelter on Chicago's West-side. After finishing my sermon, before I took my seat, the director's daughter prophesied to my wife and I saying that we would be publishing children's books. During the drive back home, we discussed the prophecy. We both concluded this prophesy was way off because we were in the social services business at the time, not publishing. However, five years later, after helping a friend get his book published, I started my own publishing company. Eight years after starting our publishing company, we published our first children's book in 2018, fourteen years after it was prophesied.

What's interesting about this story is, I didn't know the director's daughter had a prophetic gift. She didn't call herself a prophetess. We were not at a church. We were not at some prophetic conference. This was spontaneous and unexpected, but God directed. Both my wife and I will be the first to admit, we I did not take her words seriously because the prophecy seemed baseless. It wasn't until I was uploading the elements of a children's book to the manufacturer that God brought back to my remembrance, of that prophetic word we received fourteen years earlier. I recently I spoke with this woman and told her that the prophecy has been fulfilled. She was just as amazed as I was.

THE MESSAGE OF THE PROPHET

Prophecy is probably the most intriguing among the various forms of biblical literature. As a whole, prophecy should not be viewed merely as a collection of predictions of gloom and doom or God's displeasure and anger at his people or the world, but its messages are also encouraging, strengthening, and filled with blessing and hope. However, in giving these messages, the purposes and plan of God and the character and personality of the prophet become enmeshed. Even though it is God's message, it's the prophet's person in which the people see and interact. It is through the prophet's character, emotions, disposition and experience in which God's prophetic word must come through. Therefore, just as a tree is known by its fruit, so a prophet is known by his prophetic messages. Though people may not accept the message or the messenger, they recognize that a legitimate prophet speaks on the behalf of the Lord.

Since prophets are God's mouthpiece, this often put the prophet in a precarious situation with the people. In the following passage, here is what God told Jeremiah:

> *Prophecies that are of human origin do not have heaven's perspective, and they cannot discern the secrets of men's heart. They are limited to a message that entices people about materialism and wealth, but bring no conviction of sin.*

> But they did not obey or incline their ear, but walked in their own counsels and the stubbornness of their evil hearts, and went backward and not forward. From the day that your fathers came out of the land of Egypt to this day, I have persistently sent all my servants the prophets to them, day after day. Yet they did not listen to me or incline their ear, but stiffened their neck. They did worse than their fathers. "So you shall speak all these words to them, but they will not listen to you. You shall call to them, but they will not answer you.
>
> Jeremiah 7:24-27, ESV

Prophets had the formidable task of delivering a word from the Lord that in many cases was particularly unfavorable to stiff-necked people. Prophets were often shunned, rejected and even killed. Though ultimately it was God and His message that the people were rejecting, it was the prophet, God's messenger, that caught the brunt of the people's complaint and anger. Calling out people's wickedness is dangerous business. Decrying the failing of a corrupt political system and priesthood could get the prophet killed. In the Gospels, Jesus lamented this very fact when He said:

> O Jerusalem, Jerusalem, the city that kills the prophets and stones those who are sent to it! How often would I have gathered your children together as a hen gathers her brood under her wings, and you were not willing!
>
> Matthew 23:37, ESV

This passage gives a glimpse at the heart of God who only wanted to save, protect, and bless His people that He loved so much. But instead of heeding God's voice, they vented their anger at the prophet. Their hostile action towards the prophet was the manifestation of their wicked hearts that were opposed to God's righteousness and rule.

In Jeremiah 7:25, God gave Jeremiah some historical insight as to Israel's rejection of Himself, when he made reference to the Exodus, where God tested Israel during their forty-year journey through the wilderness to the Promised Land. One would think after four-hundred years in slavery and finally being delivered by a barrage of miraculous events that broke the Egyptians' back, that Israel would want God to communicate directly to them; however, that was not the case. In Exodus 20, we find what the children of Israel said to Moses:

> Speak to us yourself and we will listen. But do not have
> God speak to us or we will die. Moses said to the people,
> Do not be afraid. God has come to test you, so that the
> fear of God will be with you to keep you from sinning.
> Exodus 20:19-20

There are a few reasons why this passage is important. The first reason is because the people did not want God to talk to them directly because they were terrified of Him—but why? From the very beginning, Adam and Eve became afraid of God, only after they had fallen into sin. Sin has always been the issue between God and man. Not only did sin separate us from God, it also made us afraid of Him, because sin carries guilt and the fear of judgment. This is why Adam and Eve hid themselves when the Lord called out to them in the Garden. Moses attempted to appeal to the people by reasoning with them. In a sense he was saying, "Come on, don't be afraid of the Lord! He's putting the fear of God in you so you won't keep sinning." Not sinning was the only way to have God's favor and blessing to abide upon Israel.

Again, sin is the problem. Isaiah so passionately appeals to God's people when he says: "But your iniquities have separated you from your God; your sins have hidden his face from you, so that he will not hear"(Isaiah 59:2). It is sin that has always been the barrier to God's blessing. Where there is no sin, there is unfettered fellowship and access to God. The ultimate expression of that is in heaven, where God Himself will dwell with his people (Rev. 21:3).This is how it was in the beginning, where we see God in the cool of the day coming to fellowship with Adam and Eve. However, after sinning, Adam and Eve hid themselves from God's presence (Gen. 3:8).

Once sin entered into the picture, the dynamics of the relationship between God and man changed drastically. The fact that man was now separated from God's presence altered every aspect of God's relationship with man. Now that man was irreversibly tainted by sin, the only way for people to approach God was by way of a blood sacrifice subsequently creating the need for a priest and priesthood. Again, since separation had occurred where communication and fellowship with man were also severed, this eventually created the need for a prophet. When there is direct access to God, a prophet is no longer necessary. Once we are in heaven, prophecy shall cease (1 Cor. 13:8).

During the Church age, the Holy Spirit is given to indwell believers, to sanctify, empower them, and to lead and guide them into all truth. This was not the case prior to Pentecost. In the Old Testament, the Spirit rested *upon* God's people to empower them for service, though there is a reference to the Spirit of Christ being in the prophets of old (1 Peter1:11). But now we are His temple where the Spirit takes up residency as He perfects our holiness. How effective this sanctifying process is depends upon a Christian's maturity, knowledge in the Lord, and submission to God's will. A Christian that attends a good church with a pastor that is walking in the will of the Lord does not need to consult with someone who carries the title of prophet.

Understanding the purpose for a prophet helps us better understand the purpose behind a true prophetic message that always originates from God's frame of reference and is given according to His righteousness and holiness. The God who knows all things, fills all time and space, and has all power is very desirous for His people to be in relationship with Him so that His people can experience the blessing of having God's goodness and mercy abide upon them. Therefore, God is very concerned about *anything* that would impede the flow of His favor and grace to His people. Since God cannot tolerate sin and wickedness, the number one impediment of God's blessing and favor, He sends his prophet with a message of rebuke and repentance to the world, a nation, a king, to the masses, or to an individual so that repentance, reconciliation, and restoration can occur.

Prophecies that are of human origin do not have heaven's perspective, and they cannot discern the secrets of men's heart. They are limited to a message that entices people about materialism and wealth, but brings no conviction of sin. True prophecy originates from the heart and mind of a sagacious God, who knows perfectly the hearts of men, all things of the world, and all knowledge of the future. God's message would have men to align with His righteousness and His Kingdom. Therefore, the prophetic message that is divine conflicts with the desires of a wicked human heart that is attuned to the things of this world. This is why the prophetic message is typically so burdensome, and brings tension and persecution to the prophet bearing God's message.

In Jeremiah 23:29, God spoke these words: "Is not My word like a fire?" says the LORD, "And like a hammer *that* breaks the rock in pieces"(NKJV)? God's word was like a hammer because that's what it took to break up the hardness of the people's stony heart that refused to heed Jehovah's message to repent. Instead, they would rather be deceived by the appeasing messages of false prophets who never addressed their sins. Again, Jeremiah says:

> Your prophets have predicted for you falsehood and delusion *and* foolish things; and they have not exposed your

iniquity *and* guilt to avert your captivity [by causing you
to repent]. But they have divined *and* declared to you
false *and* deceptive prophecies, worthless *and* misleading.

Lamentations 2:14, AMP

This passage puts clear emphasis on what I have covered thus far by identifying what happens when a false prophet's message is heeded as opposed to a true prophet. As we have discovered, a true prophet's message would deal with the people's sin, which would have caused them to repent and avert consequences and judgment. But instead, the people did not want to hear from the only God who could save them. No, they wanted to be told a good, soothing message saying "everything is gonna be all right. Goodness and prosperity to you and yours," when in actuality, disaster was on the way. Ironically, false prophets never seem to be able to predict the disaster that comes to those who rebel against God and heed their lying prophecies.

MICAIAH THE PROPHET

In the 22ⁿᵈ chapter of 1 Kings, we find a very interesting account that gives us some more insight into the message of a true prophet. After approximately three years of peace between Israel and Syria, King Ahab had conceived the idea of recapturing Ramoth-Gilead from the Syrians. Jehoshaphat, King of Judah, expressed a willingness to help Ahab in this military campaign. However, Jehoshaphat suggested that before going into battle, Ahab should seek the Lord through a prophet.

In keeping with Jehoshaphat's advice, Ahab sought the counsel from four-hundred prophets of *his own* court. It is interesting that false prophets appear in large numbers. This is typical of human reasoning that puts trust in numbers as a show of force. If you get enough people saying the same thing, it will quickly be accepted as truth because it comes from the majority opinion. All these prophets advised in favor of Ahab's idea, saying, "Go," they answered, "for the Lord will give it into the king's hand" (verse 6). However, Jehoshaphat wasn't buying it. Clearly, Jehoshaphat knew that Ahab's prophets were false prophets and could not be trusted. He then asked if there was a prophet *of the Lord* which they could consult. This brought up Micaiah, a true and courageous prophet of the Lord, but Ahab hated him. Here is why:

> But Jehoshaphat said, "Is there not yet a prophet of the LORD here, that we may inquire of him?" And the king of Israel said to Jehoshaphat, "There is yet one man by whom we may inquire of the LORD, but I hate him, because he does not prophesy good concerning me, but evil. He is Micaiah son of Imlah." But Jehoshaphat said, "Let not the king say so."
>
> 1 Kings 22:7-8, NASB

As we have covered earlier, a true prophet is God's mouthpiece. Therefore, the prophet receives his message from an all-knowing God that sees and knows everything. The Lord's primary objective when giving prophetic message is not to appease or entertain people, but is to reveal truth and righteousness in the earth realm according to God's purposes and plans. Again, this is why a true prophet's message was not typically favorable, because people are typically out of the will of God. God's ways are not our ways! He is not a man that he should lie. Ahab knew that whenever Micaiah prophesied to him, the prophet was going to tell the truth.

Unlike his four-hundred false prophets whose agenda was to appease the king with lying prophecies, Micaiah's prophecies came from the Lord, and were correct and called out wickedness. Truthfully speaking, a wicked person can only receive unfavorable prophecy from a righteous prophet, because true prophecy would deal with their sin. Ahab hated Micaiah because Ahab and Jezebel were wicked rulers. The ungodly particularly despise the message of a true prophet, because they are always out of the will of God. It is never God's agenda to appease people with pacifying prophecies, but rather to bring people to repentance for His righteousness sake.

> *The world's message will always be centered upon, a bigger, a better, a brighter you, by doing it the world's way, not God's way. This is true even when the methods and message are packaged in Christian terminology, imagery, or even done in the name of the Lord.*

DO YOU COME IN PEACE?

The way people viewed a true prophet of the Lord ranged from reverence and respect all the way to outright hatred. However, in 1 Samuel 16, we find how the elders of Bethlehem responded to Samuel's arrival:

> Samuel did what the LORD said. When he arrived at Bethlehem, the elders of the town trembled when they met him. They asked, "Do you come in peace?"
>
> 1 Samuel 16:4

This passage gives us an insight into how people responded to the prophet. Notice it does not say the elders of the city rejoiced to see Samuel coming, nor did they come out with pomp and circumstance. There were no red carpets nor the sounding of trumpets. No, what they did is trembled. This begs the question, why would they tremble at the coming of a prophet? People certainly do not do that today. People are in lines that stretch around the block and fill up churches to capacity just to be tantalized by some so-called prophet to give "a word" that God is going to bless them. The only reason why people would want to see a prophet is to hear some good news or some prediction of future fortune or blessing—which amounts to nothing more than fortunetelling (more on this later).

Conversely, no one wants to be around a prophet that hears from the Lord who will call out people's sin from the pulpit to the pews. Churches far and few in between would welcome a prophet that can reveal the things that the Spirit searches, even the deep, hidden things of the heart. No, the Bethlehem elders trembled because prophets revealed the mind of God, as God searched the hearts and actions of the people. They asked if he came in peace because prophets pronounced God's chastisement and judgment. God is primarily concerned with people living righteously so that He may bless and fulfill His covenant to them. The question "do you come in peace" can be interpreted as asking, "Is everything all right?" "Are we in trouble?" "Is God displeased with something and sent you to reveal it?" This is why the elders who came to meet Samuel trembled, because being uncovered by a prophet and being under God's judgment was a traumatic experience.

GOD KNOWS THE PLANS HE HAS FOR YOU

In Jeremiah 29, the Lord makes this passionate statement: "For I know the plans I have for you," declares the LORD, "plans to prosper you and not to harm you, plans to give you hope and a future" (Jer. 29:11). This is probably one of the most preached passages from the book of Jeremiah. On any given Sunday, pastors all over the country are using this passage to encourage God's people. However, the context of this passage finds Judah captive in Babylon for their national sins and backsliding.

In approximately 605 B.C., Nebuchadnezzar besieged and destroyed Jerusalem, something that was long prophesied to take place (i.e., Isaiah, Jeremiah, Habakkuk, etc.). However, Judah refused to heed God's prophetic warning that judgment would come if they did not repent. In Jeremiah 29, exile and captivity had already occurred. Therefore, Jeremiah wrote a letter to those who were now captive in Babylon telling them to settle down, plant vineyards, let your sons and daughters marry, and be productive, because they were going to be there for a long time—seventy years to be exact (Jer. 25:11). Though the circumstance that they were in was because of God's national chastisement, in the midst of captivity, God was yet giving them hope.

In Jehovah's passionate appeal to His people, he assures them that *"He knows* the plans that he has for his people." This is the point that cannot be over emphasized. God is the planner. He's the one with the plans, not us! God knows and controls the future, we don't! Therefore, it is God who then communicates these plans to and through His prophet. In this passage, God reveals that His future intentions are to "prosper you and give you hope and a future," but it requires right standing with God. In verse 12-13, the Lord goes on the say:

> Then you will call on me and come and pray to me, and I will listen to you. You will seek me and find me when you seek me with all your heart. I will be found by you," declares the LORD, "and will bring you back from captivity...."

Since it is God who is the blesser, who knows all things and knows the path that people will take, therefore, He also knows the danger of the bad decisions you are making. To prevent us from making shipwreck, He sends a prophetic word of correction so we will change direction. God would not have sent Judah into captivity had they repented! The Babylonian captivity was a response to Judah's callous heart. One of the most loving acts that God can do is to forewarn us of consequences to come if we refuse to change.

In all of this we are learning that one of the principal purposes for the prophetic message is so people can know the heart of God. He truly wants what is best for us. He so much wants to bless us, not to harm us. He has some wonderful plans to give you hope and a fulfilling future. The question is, why won't people heed the prophetic message? Why don't people simply say, "God just wants this for my good, so I'm gonna change, get it right so God can bless me." The answer is because people have "desperately wicked hearts." Jeremiah illuminates the depth of wickedness of the heart when he states: "The heart *is* deceitful above all *things,* And desperately wicked; Who can know it" (Jer.17:9, NKJV)? "Who can know it" means that we cannot comprehend the depth of our own wickedness! From our perspective, we are just fine. But David asked, "But who can discern their own errors? Forgive my hidden faults" (Psalm 19:12).

Since we have wicked hearts, our propensity and proclivities are bent towards sin and the things that please the flesh. It is through the desires of the flesh that we connect with the cares of this world, from where the lust of the flesh, the lust of the eye, and the pride of life permeate and dominate (see 1 John 2:16). Therefore, if our primary motivations in life are driven by the world, the flesh, and the devil, a prophetic message that implores people to come out from the ways of the world would be rejected. This is the reason Jesus stated, "No one can serve two masters; for either he will hate the one and love the other, or he will be devoted to one and despise the other. You cannot serve God and wealth" (Matt.6:24, NASB).

Money allows us access to participate in what the world offers. Having a home, food, and shelter are indeed necessities that take money to obtain. God does not have a problem with that in and of itself. But it is *the love of money* that is the root of all evil (1 Tim. 6:10). Those who are of the world are seeking money first and all the things it can buy, so that they may satisfy the lust of the flesh, the lust of the eye, and the pride of life. These are the principles on which much of the world is based. But the prophetic message says, "For all that is in the world—the desires of the flesh and the desires of the eyes and pride of life—is not from the Father but is from the world" (1 John 2:16, ESV). Therefore, the world's message will always be centered upon a bigger, a better, a brighter you, by doing it the world's way, not God's way. This is true even when the world's methods and message are packaged in Christian terminology, imagery, or even done in the name of the Lord. We are warned, "Do not love the world or anything in the world. If anyone loves the world, love for the Father is not in them" (1 John 2:15). False prophets are so dangerous because their message will lead you away from God, to compromise and embrace the world while with their lips they promote Christ. "These people honor me with their lips, but their hearts are far from me. They worship me in vain; their teachings are merely human rules" (Matt.15:8-9).

We are admonished, "Do not conform to the pattern of this world, but be transformed by the renewing of your mind. Then you will be able to test and approve what God's will is—his good, pleasing and perfect will" (Rom.12:2). God's will for you is "*good, pleasing* and *perfect.*" *Good* for you from His righteous perspective. *Pleasing* to Him because He's the author and perfecter of our faith, and *perfect* because He has designed it specifically for you. All this is so you will not be seduced by the enticements of this world and pulled off course, or be deceived by a false prophecy that redirects your affections towards this world.

The Lord addressed this very subject when instructing his disciples. In Matthew 6:24, the Lord had already taught that you cannot serve both God and money. Jesus goes on to say:

> For this reason I say to you do not be worried about your life, *as to* what you will eat or what you will drink; nor for your body, *as to* what you will put on. Is not life more than food, and the body more than clothing? Do not worry then, saying, 'What will we eat?' or 'What will we drink?' or 'What will we wear for clothing?' "For the Gentiles eagerly seek all these things; for your heavenly Father knows that you need all these things."But seek first His kingdom and His righteousness, and all these things will be added to you."
>
> Matthew 6:25-33, NASB

Here, Jesus is making a clear difference between the cares and dictates of the world and the principles of the kingdom of God—they are diametrically opposed! For those that have no relationship with God, the most important thing in life is fulfilling the lust of the flesh through materialism (pursuit of wealth) and hedonism (the pursuit of pleasure). When an individual has no relationship with God, there is no expectation of eternity. Their philosophy is simply "eat, drink and be merry, for tomorrow we die." When there is no expectation of judgment, then everyone does what is right in his own eyes. To this ideology Jesus responded, saying, "For the Gentiles (or non-believers) eagerly seek all these things." People who are motivated by money and materialism are not hearing from God, they are hearing from the world.

However, the true prophetic message would be, God already knows what you need, and is in a much better position to supply your needs, because He knows your beginning and ending and has ordered your footsteps. Therefore, you should first seek the kingdom of God and his "righteousness." Remember, it is always going to be God's agenda to assure that people are in right standing with Him. He says that if you will seek God with all your heart, and hunger after His righteousness, and turn from your wicked ways, He will add the things that your heart desires. It is actually folly to assume that you need to inform God of your needs, when He knows that better than you do. God can bless you to such a degree that you won't have room to receive it, but you must seek His kingdom and His righteousness. This is what the core of God's prophetic message to His people has always been, whether it be individually, nationally, or politically. The righteousness of God is being revealed from heaven from faith to faith. He knows the plans that he has for you, to do you good, not to harm you but to bring you to a fulfilling future.

COME SEE A MAN!

For the final leg of this study, we must come to the Gospel of John, where Jesus encounters a Samaritan woman where they have both come to draw water from Jacob's well. What we find here is another powerful prophetic message, not based upon anything about this woman's future, but about specifics concerning her past. The text reads as follows:

> Jesus said to her, "Go, call your husband, and come here." The woman answered and said, "I have no hus-

band." Jesus said to her, "You have well said, 'I have no husband,' for you have had five husbands, and the one whom you now have is not your husband; in that you spoke truly." The woman said to Him, "Sir, I perceive that You are a prophet."

John 4:16-19, NKJV

Once again, we have a clear example concerning the essence of a prophetic message, but this time from Jesus in the New Testament. From the vantage point of the times in which Jesus lived, the Jews knew the signs of a true prophet. Whether it was powerful, miraculous signs like raising the dead (Luke 7:16) or having word of knowledge to discern a person's life (Luke 7:39), the signs of a prophet were well known to the people. It was no different for this woman from Sychar, a town in Samaria. After encountering this unnamed woman at Jacob's well, Jesus demonstrated His love for this woman as He prioritized her spiritual needs over her physical needs. Asking her to go call her husband was a setup for him to expose the sin in her life and to introduce her to eternal life.

It is interesting to note the specificity of the Lord's prophetic discernment. He told her how many husbands she had, and called her out on the fact that the man she was now living with was not her husband. The Lord was not vague by saying, "There are some things going on in your life," or "You are having some issues with your relationships." No, the Lord was unmistakably specific. On the other hand, false prophets tend to be notoriously vague (more on this later). Neither did Jesus enter into a prognosticative dialogue about some fortune in this woman's near future (something on which false prophets readily focus). But by prophesying specific truth, dealing directly with her sin, he established his office as a true prophet, and the Samaritan woman knew it. Jesus did not have to declare himself to be the prophet; after His prophesying to her, she made that declaration herself. Today's prophets always have to declare themselves to be a prophet. She knew that everything

He said about her was the truth. Only a true prophet could have possibly known how many husbands she had over the span of her life in Samaria, a place and a people that the Jews detested.

Even though her sin had been uncovered, her encounter with Jesus was not shaming, but liberating. This goes to the point that there are people who know that they are sinners and know the life that they are living is wrong. When their sin is uncovered, they want to repent and be free, but people with hard hearts become infuriated and attack the prophet for telling the truth. But after her encounter with the Lord, her mission and her testimony had been changed. Back to Samaria she went, without her water pots she so hastily left behind, but with a message of hope, saying "Come see a man...."

It should not be lost that in verse 4, it says that Jesus "must needs go to Samaria" (KJV), because as some assert, it was the preferred route the Jews would take heading north from Judea to Galilee. However, I believe there was a spiritual reason He took this route. Since Jesus was coming from where John was baptizing, which was in Aenon near Salim (John 3:23) in the Jordon Valley, going to Samaria from there was more a geographical detour than a convenient route.[6] Jesus was on a mission, and He knew that He would meet this woman who was from a place and a people long rejected by the Jews. As a matter of fact, when He sent out his disciples He forbade them to go to Samaria (Matt. 10:5). However, this encounter was obviously important to His messianic mission to seek and save that which was lost.

When this Samaritan woman returned to her country, undoubtedly she spread the news about Jesus, the same country where just a few years later, Philip the evangelist would be preaching the Gospel and saving many souls. And the same place where an ominous figure named *Simon the Sorcerer* would be encountered.

And the LORD said to me: "The prophets are prophesying lies in my name. I did not send them, nor did I command them or speak to them. They are prophesying to you a lying vision, worthless divination, and the deceit of their own minds.
Jeremiah 14:14, ESV

Chapter 2

Spinning a Web of Deception

Simon Magus

Simon, a certain Samaritan of the village of Githon, was one of the number, who, in the reign of Claudius Caesar, performed many magic rites by the operation of demons...

Eusebius' Ecclesiastical History[7]

In the book of Acts, Dr. Luke introduces us to an enigmatic, shadowy figure historically referred to as *Simon the Sorcerer*, who wielded great influence in Samaria. The passage below sets the stage for us to begin our study.

> There was a certain man called Simon, who previously practiced sorcery in the city and astonished the people of Samaria, claiming that he was someone great, to whom they all gave heed, from the least to the greatest, saying, "This man is the great power of God." And they heeded him because he had astonished them with his sorceries for a long time.
>
> Acts 8:9-11, NKJV

As the text informs us, Samaria was under Simon's influence. The people highly regarded him because for a long time he had *bewitched* them with his *sorcery*. The word *bewitched* comes from the Greek word, *existēmi*,[8] which means *"to be amazed, astonished, to be put out of wits."* To put it in today's vernacular, it means to be completely "blown away," to be shocked, stunned, or flabbergasted. The impact of Simon's mystical proficiency that held the Samaritans in awe and contributed to his extensive influence was because of his use of sorcery. The definition of *sorcery* is *"the use of supernatural power over others through the assistance of spirits…."*[9] According to *Eusebius*, Simon's source of power was demonic.[10] This was why he was able to hold sway over so many people. An example of this seductive power can be seen in Acts 8:9, where Simon is promoting himself as *"Someone Great."* In verse 10, we see the extent of Simon's influence, "to whom they all gave heed, from the least to the greatest, saying, 'This man is the great power of God'" (Acts 8:10, NKJV). Herein is the problem. Simon practiced sorcery! He operated under the influence of demons! Yet the people exclaimed, "This man is the great power of God!"

Simon was bewitching them through hell's power, but the people attributed it to heaven's power. At this point, I must emphasize that all things supernatural are not all things Godly. Demons are spirits, therefore everything they do is supernatural too. Whether it is to empower through sorcery or divination (more on divination later), it's all supernatural. Just because something is supernatural, does not mean it is holy or inspired by the Holy Spirit. This is why those who are *sign seekers* must be wary, because they are more susceptible to being pulled into the abyss of deception.

SIMON'S SORCERY

Let's return to our examination of Simon the Sorcerer. Though the Scriptures do not state explicitly what was the range of Simon's power, we do know it caused him to have great influence over the people. Whenever someone exercises too much influence over people, corruption and disaster soon follow. This is why the old axiom warns: *Power corrupts, and absolute power corrupts absolutely*. Too often, we have seen the tragic results when an individual exercises too much control over peo-

> *Simon's attraction to Philip's ministry was not because he loved Jesus or Philip's preaching. Simon was attracted to the miracles not the message. This is still a problem today.*
>
>

ple's lives. The Samaritans of old believed that Simon was *" . . . the Great Power of God."* Unfortunately, time has not made an improvement in people's discernment. In this sense, many of today's Christians are like the Samaritans of old.

Though Satan spins his web of deception, it's the lack of knowledge that gets people caught. Hence the Scripture *"My People are destroyed for lack of knowledge"* is a solemn warning against the devastating effects of ignorance (Hosea 4:6). People who are not knowledgeable in the word of God cannot discern the difference between God and the subtlety of Satan, which can cause someone to attribute to God the works that are really from the Devil.

PHILIP THE EVANGELIST

Now let's switch focus briefly to a godly and highly anointed man named Philip, also known as Philip the Evangelist. He too, was in Samaria, but he was proclaiming the Gospel of Jesus Christ, and his ministry was authenticated by signs and wonders.

> Then Philip went down to the city of Samaria and preached Christ to them. And the multitudes with one accord heeded the things spoken by Philip, hearing and seeing the miracles which he did. For unclean spirits, crying with a loud voice, came out of many who were possessed; and many who were paralyzed and lame were healed. And there was great joy in that city.
>
> Acts 8:5-8, NKJV

As the book of Acts declares, Philip the Evangelist was declaring the Gospel of Jesus Christ. But he wasn't only declaring, he came forth with the demonstration of power, with signs and wonders. Verse 6 reads "…the multitudes with one accord heeded the things spoken by Philip, hearing and seeing the miracles which he did." As a result, the Samaritans were gladly receiving the good news of the Gospel and being saved. While all of this was occurring, Simon was beholding the miracles that Philip performed and was attracted to his display of power. In the midst of this ancient evangelistic crusade, here is what Simon did:

> But when they believed Philip as he preached the things concerning the kingdom of God and the name of Jesus Christ, both men and women were baptized. Then Simon himself also *believed*; and when he **was baptized he continued with Philip,** and was amazed, seeing the miracles and signs which were done. (Emphasis mine)
>
> Acts 8:12-13, NKJV

This is incredible! Simon responded to an altar call and stepped right up and confessed his belief in Jesus Christ. Then he went to the next step of his public confession and got baptized. After his baptism, Simon continued on with Philip. Verse 13 of the *Amplified Bible* says it this way, "…and after being baptized, devoted himself constantly to him. And seeing signs *and* miracles of great power which were being performed, he was utterly amazed." After being baptized, Simon *devoted himself constantly* to Philip. So now we have a situation where a sorcerer heard the Gospel message, believed, and got baptized in the name of the Lord Jesus Christ. Finally, he even traveled along with Philip's evangelistic ministry. For all practical purposes, Simon joined Philip's ministry. So Simon, who practiced sorcery before meeting Philip, was now a Christian. Or was he?

Going back to Matthew 7:21, where Jesus declares: "Not everyone that saith unto me Lord, Lord, shall enter into the kingdom of Heaven..." Yes, it is true the Scriptures say that Simon believed, and was baptized. But, as we will see later, he wasn't saved. Questions concerning legitimate conversions have always presented a dilemma to the ministry. It can be a real problem distinguishing those among you who are real and those who are not. As the text implies, many people believed and were baptized. Who's going to doubt someone's sincerity who comes to the altar after hearing the Gospel message? What pastor today would do that? There is no evidence in this passage that anyone doubted Simon's sincerity—not even Philip! Philip obviously permitted Simon to come along with him. We know that Simon believed the Gospel. We know that he was baptized by Philip in the name of Jesus Christ. We know that he continued along with Philip, but here is what happened next.

After the news reached Jerusalem that the Samaritans had received the word of God, they sent for the apostles Peter and John to come to Samaria. Their mission was to go down to Samaria and pray for those who received Christ, so that they might also receive the Holy Spirit. When the apostles arrived, they did just that. As the passage tells us, when the apostles laid their hands on the believers, they received the Holy Spirit (Acts 8:14-17). Though the Scriptures do not say that those who received the Holy Spirit prophesied or spoke in tongues, I believe there was a powerful manifestation of the Holy Spirit. Evidently, whatever Simon witnessed as people received the Holy Spirit, it obviously impressed him:

> When Simon saw that the Spirit was given at the laying on of the apostles' hands, he offered them money and said, "Give me also this ability so that everyone on whom I lay my hands may receive the Holy Spirit." Peter answered: "May your money perish with you, because you thought you could buy the gift of God with money! You have no part or share in this ministry, because your heart is not right before God. Repent of this

> *If God has a word for you, He knows where you are. He knows how to speak to you. You don't have to run to and fro to hear "a word" from a so-called prophet.*

wickedness and pray to the Lord in the hope that he may forgive you for having such a thought in your heart. For I see that you are full of bitterness and captive to sin." Then Simon answered, "Pray to the Lord for me so that nothing you have said may happen to me.

Acts 8:18-24

Simon's statement indicates that he was interested in only one thing, promoting himself as being *"The great power of God."* Simon obviously saw the power of the Spirit moving in these believers, so now he wanted another trick to add to his repertoire of enchantments. When Simon said this, he revealed the true intentions of his heart. As Jesus said, "Brood of vipers! How can you, being evil, speak good things? For out of the abundance of the heart the mouth speaks"(Matthew 12:34, NKJV). Indeed, not only did Simon say a mouthful, he said a heart full!

If I may digress briefly and return to verse 13, the passage begins to paint a clear picture of what was really motivating Simon all the time. The verse says: "…and when he was baptized he continued with Philip, and was amazed, seeing the miracles and signs which were done." From this passage, we may conclude that Simon's attraction to Philip's ministry was not because he loved Jesus or Philip's preaching. Simon was attracted to the *miracles*, not the *message*. This is still a problem today. When people experience fantastic occurrences such as miracles, they can become so intrigued they may agree to or affirm anything. These types of professions may not be genuine, because they are made from the basis of ecstatic emotions. An example of this can be found in John chapter 2, beginning at verse 23. The passage says:

> Now when He was in Jerusalem at the Passover, during the feast, many believed in His name when they saw the signs which He did. But Jesus did not commit Himself to them, because He knew all *men*, and had no need that anyone should testify of man, for He knew what was in man.
>
> John 2:23-25, NKJV

In this passage we have a clear example of those who, after seeing miracles, were confessing belief in Christ. However, Jesus would not commit himself to them, because he knew their hearts. These people were only seeking the sensational and spectacular, and so it was with Simon the sorcerer. There was never any genuine content in his profession of faith:

> Peter answered: "May your money perish with you, because you thought you could buy the gift of God with money! You have no part or share in this ministry, because your heart is not right before God."
>
> Acts 8:20-21

Since Simon probably achieved wealth from utilizing his mystical powers, in his mind at least, buying the Holy Spirit would be a good investment. He wanted the ability to impart the Holy Spirit on whomever he laid his hands on, so he could charge them. Simon was looking at the power, influence, and wealth that this could bring to him. Influence over people and acquiring wealth was always the primary motivating factor for false prophets back then, as it is today. It's all about the money (more on this later).

I find it very interesting that of the many things that Dr. Luke recorded in Acts, he included these encounters with Simon Magus. Since it is true that all Scripture was given by inspiration, and is profitable for instruction, then a question we need to ask ourselves is, How might today's Christian be instructed concerning these matters? If Peter and John had not come to Samaria, how far might Simon have gone in

> *Counterfeit Charisma are those gifts, that imitate the spiritual gifts empowered by the Holy Spirit but are inspired by the powers of darkness, and are phony, but only in the sense that their source is not the Holy Spirit which it imitates.*

posing as a Christian? But even more intriguing is this question, If Simon were looking for a church home today, where would he look? What church fellowships and congregations would he fit in? Which churches would allow Simon access to their pulpits and congregations? Which churches are so desirous of signs and wonders that Simon's sorcery would be interpreted as a display of God's power just as it was in Samaria?

It is for this very reason that pastors must be vigilant and diligent to guard against wolves sneaking in among the flock. Christians must be cautious about seeking signs, wonders, and the supernatural. Yes, God is supernatural. However, we need to be on guard against attributing all supernatural manifestations to God. In the book of Hebrews, the writer admonished those ancient Christians two-thousand years ago, and the same truth applies to us today. Those who are unskilled in the word of righteousness are not able to discern good from evil (Hebrews 5:13-14, KJV). As the apostle John warns us in his first epistle, "Beloved, do not believe every spirit, but test the spirits, whether they are of God; because many false prophets have gone out into the world" (1 John 4:1, NKJV).

Without trying the spirits, people will attribute the work of Satan to God. This is the mistake that the Samaritans made. One must understand that discernment of demonic spirits does not happen by itself. Christians must be sober and vigilant, purposeful, intentional, and unrelenting in their spiritual growth. It's not about the personalities that so many clamor after to go hear "a word" from some "so-called" prophet. If God has a word for you, He knows where you are. He knows how to speak to you. You don't have to run *to and fro* to hear "a word from the Lord." Remember, it's not about the people that you hear the word from, but it is about the Lord that gives the word. Ultimately, our battle is not with people, but against principalities, powers, and spiritual wickedness in high places. This is why we need to put on the whole armor of God so we can stand against the schemes of the devil.

As biblical prophecy asserts, there are still some Simons around who are endued with varying degrees of counterfeit charisma. One can find them practicing their magical arts on theatrical stages, or even consult with them on numerous psychic reading outlets in communities and online. These are the obvious black arts practitioners. However, there is another, more insidious breed of mystics that are difficult to distinguish. This is because they have crept into the Church and function among the sheep. One might find them ministering behind pulpits or sitting on sanctuary pews. Their voices are heard on both Christian programming and secular and religious stations. Millions view their images seen on television and the internet. False prophets perform miraculous works, they are prophesying, and they're casting out devils, all in the name of Jesus—but they are impostors.

CHARISMA AND MIRACLES

We need to ask ourselves, what is it about certain people that capture our interest the most? Is it their personality or their intelligence? Is it their oratory skills, their gift to inspire or persuade? Why do certain individuals have such an irresistible magnetism that people just hang on their every word or action? The term that describes this magnetism phenomenon is *charismatic*, an adjective deriving from its root, *charisma*. *Charisma* comes from the Greek word *charisma*, which is translated as *"gift(s)"* in the New Testament (i.e., 1 Cor. 12:4). It is defined as: a (divine) *gratuity*, i.e., *deliverance*, a (spiritual) *endowment*, i.e., a religious *qualification*, or miraculous *faculty*.[11] It is used approximately twenty-one times in the New Testament in both singular and plural forms. Of those usages, the translators added a few for clarification purposes that are italicized in the *King James Version*. From its usage in Scripture, we can conclude that God certainly has dispersed *gifts* throughout the Body of Christ, the Church. However, only chosen vessels like Philip, Peter, Paul, and others operated in supernatural gifts of healing and deliverance. And there is evidence of miracles being performed by others, because Paul asked the Galatians, "Therefore He who supplies the Spirit to you and works miracles among you, *does He do it* by the works of the law, or by the hearing of faith" (Gal.3:5, NKJV)?

The *Easton Bible Dictionary* defines a *miracle* as:

> An event in the external world brought about by the immediate agency or the simple volition of God, operating without the use of means capable of being discerned by the senses, and designed to authenticate the divine commission of a religious teacher and the truth of his message… Miracles are seals of a divine mission. The sacred writers appealed to them as proofs that they were messengers of God.[12]

From the above definition, the working of miracles or signs and wonders has a very important purpose. At times God used them to authenticate his servants. In John 3:2, Nicodemus' profession of Jesus' miraculous faculty is telling when he states: "…for no one can do these signs that You do unless God is with him."Another example of miraculous displays for authentication purposes is found in Exodus 4:1-9, where an apprehensive Moses was uncertain about the people believing that he had spoken to God. To put Moses' anxiety and the people's skepticism to rest, God gave Moses three miraculous signs: the sign of the leprous hand, his rod becoming a serpent, and water from the river turning into blood when poured out onto dry ground. God knew that these signs would authenticate Moses' calling and message. Also, in the book of Acts, Peter reasoned with the skeptics by characterizing Jesus as a . . . *man approved of God among you* . . . by the many miracles, signs and wonders that he did (Acts 2:22).

God's miracles are always flawless, and in perfect conformity to His holiness. Though miracles do authenticate the servant of God, the ultimate purpose of miracles, signs, and wonders is to bring glory to God the *miracle worker*, not the person He worked the miracle through. Those whom God uses in the supernatural should never accept the credit. Even Jesus was careful to give the glory to the Father. In John 10:32, this is what the Lord said to the Pharisees, "At my Father's direction I have done many good works. For which one are you going to stone me" (John 10:32, NLT)? In Acts, Peter declared, "Fellow Israelites, why does this surprise you? Why do you stare at us as if by our own power or godliness we had made this man walk" (Acts 3:12)? The true servant of Lord will always give that glory back to God because they know that they are not the ones really performing the miracle. Besides that, God does not share His glory with another (Isa. 42:8).

Though there are well-documented miraculous works recorded in Scripture, the overwhelming majority of God's servants and prophets were not miracle workers (i.e., the major and minor prophets). Throughout biblical history, the working of miracles was reserved for a very few. But having said that, I do believe that God works in mysterious ways today, and that there are those who have been delivered and healed miraculously somewhere on this earth every day. The following is an example.

On March 10th, 2015, a woman in Utah drove through the guard railing of a bridge that passed over a river. The car flipped over and was mostly submerged under water, some believe for up to fourteen hours. However, when the rescuers arrived on the scene, four of them heard a woman's voice calling out to them for help. So after they made it to the car, they found that the woman driver had been dead for several hours with the front end of the vehicle under water. They also found an eigh-teen-month-old baby that was hanging upside down in her car seat, dangling from the back seat with the rear end of the car sticking out of the water. The baby was unconscious and barely alive. There was no one in that car that could have possibly been calling for help. Yet four men testified on national news that they all heard a woman's voice calling out to them for help. The baby was rescued and survived.[13] Though none of those men gave God the glory for an obvious miracle, when my wife and I heard it, we did, as I am sure every Christian that heard this story did as well. Miracles happen when God ordains them to happen. The Lord makes this clear when He states:

> You will undoubtedly quote me this proverb: 'Physi-cian, heal yourself'—meaning, 'Do miracles here in your hometown like those you did in Capernaum.' But I tell you the truth, no prophet is accepted in his own hometown. Certainly there were many needy wid-ows in Israel in Elijah's time, when the heavens were closed for three and a half years, and a severe fam-ine devastated the land. Yet Elijah was not sent to any of them. He was sent instead to a foreigner—a wid-ow of Zarephath in the land of Sidon. And there were many lepers in Israel in the time of the prophet Eli-sha, but the only one healed was Naaman, a Syrian.
>
> Luke 4:23-27, NLT

This passage is interesting for a couple of important reasons. First, Jesus makes it clear that there was a great need amongst God's peo-ple the Israelites during the three-and-a-half-year famine. He said that there were "many widows in Israel" but God did not send his proph-et Elijah to heal any of them, but instead sent him to a foreigner, a Gentile, not an Israelite. He then reiterates that point when he then recounts Naaman, who—once again, not being an Israelite but a Syr-ian—was healed of his leprosy. Obviously, there were a number of

Israelites that had leprosy as well, but Elisha was sent to none of them. From these passages we learn that miracles are not tossed about like frisbees, but are strategic manifestations of God's power according to his own power and plans.

Though in no way am I minimizing the miracles that have occurred in the lives of God's people down through the ages all over the world. But just as the miracles that Jesus cited, the miracle in Utah wasn't witnessed by the people you would expect. The reason why I emphasize this supernatural incident is because it was well reported on CNN, Fox, and other news outlets. Secondly, this event was clearly supernatural, but it did not involve any subjective observers hidden from scrutiny in some obscure church, but occurred outside the walls of the Church in plain view with witnesses who apparently were not religious.

COUNTERFEIT CHARISMA

Throughout history, there have been many members of the clergy, politics, the corporate world, entertainers, and others, who have all possessed varying degrees of charisma. However, just because a person possesses charisma doesn't necessarily mean they're under God's anointing. According to the definition of *charismatic*, Adolf Hitler and Jim Jones were charismatic leaders causing the death of six million Jews and nine hundred followers, respectively. Both started out as charismatic leaders for a cause and found a group of people with which to connect. The people's needs mixed with a message of hope, freedom, and conquest serve as a basis to create an intoxicating charismatic atmosphere where the devil's influence is not always obvious. In 2 Corinthians 11:14, Paul warns: "And no wonder, for Satan himself masquerades as an angel of light." Therefore, anything of value, anything of importance, anything necessary makes it a candidate for counterfeiting.

The dictionary defines *counterfeit* as: "*To make a copy of, usually with the intent to defraud; forge: counterfeits money. To carry on a deception.*"[14] Counterfeits can look so real that without the proper training, you could never tell the difference. One important thing to remember about a counterfeit is that since it is not genuine, it has telltale flaws, or there is something essential missing. This is what gives it away. For example, when a Secret Service agent is examining counterfeit hundred dollar bills, he doesn't need to know all about the different counterfeit notes. All he needs to know is what a real one-hundred dollar bill looks like, feels like, all the specifications, and hidden features. The same applies to the Christian's ability to discern the spirit of truth from the spirit of error. You may not know about all the different false prophets that will come, but by knowing the Word of God, you can detect a counterfeit. This is why it is imperative that the Christian studies and is knowledgeable and knows how to rightly divine the Scriptures.

In the first book, I defined *Counterfeit Charisma* as:

> ...those gifts, that imitate the spiritual gifts empowered by the Holy Spirit that are inspired by the powers of darkness, and are phony, but only in the sense that their source is not the Holy Spirit which it imitates. They are real supernatural powers, purposed to seduce, and to deceive that manifest through counterfeit forms of spiritual gifts found in the Scriptures. These counterfeits are inspired by seducing and lying spirits, and are sought by the spiritually immature and biblically unlearned individuals and are propagated through doctrines of devils but taught by false Christians, ministers, teachers, apostles and prophets.[15]

This definition intentionally casts a wide net because of the vast array and manifold manifestations of counterfeit charisma that is so prevalent in churches and society at large. When it comes to the operation of the spiritual gifts, somewhere along the line, people are getting sidetracked and lured into a world of deception that is passing itself off as legitimate functionality when it is not. This is why this study is so critical, because these gifts are typically found in Charismatic and Pentecostal churches. However, I am not saying that all Pentecostals are errant, heretical fanatics, though there many scholars that believe just that. In his book *Charismatic Chaos*, Dr. John MacArthur asserts that if they (meaning Pentecostals and Charismatics) were honest with themselves, they would have to admit that *experience*, not the Bible, is what their belief system is based on.[16] However, this is not the position espoused in this book, because it is difficult to understand how someone can be a Christian without *experiencing* God's power in their life. Many conservative scholars believe that God does not speak to people today, but that He only communicates through the Scriptures. The only problem with that is Jesus said, "My sheep hear my voice…" (John 10:27).

At this point I must confess the idea of God speaking to people is very controversial. Many scholars espouse that since the closing of the canon of Scripture, God only speaks through the Bible. They further assert that God is not giving any "new revelation." Noted scholar J.I. Packer asserts, "God has no more to say to the world, in this age, than He says in the Scriptures…."[17] To a certain extent, I agree with that. No, God is not giving a new revelation that would result in the 151st Psalm, a 67th chapter to Isaiah, or a 23rd chapter to the book of Revelation. Certainly not! However, the God who formed man's mouth and gave him the ability to communicate intelligently, can speak to whomever and whenever He wants. God speaks through inner witness, our conscious, and through the Holy Spirit's illumination of the Scriptures as the Spirit leads and guides in all truth. Whereas care must be taken when it comes to subjective revelation, we cannot throw the baby out with the bath water, to say God hasn't spoken to anyone since the fourth century when the canon was closed. To say that God does not speak today itself is a subjective statement. Those who hold that position should more accurately state, "God has never spoken *to me*."

SIMON'S LICENTIOUS LEGACY

So whatever happened to Simon Magus? Luke doesn't give us any more information about him in Acts. However, there are several historic accounts of Simon and his heretical legacy. Ancient philosopher and apologist Justin Martyr records that during the reign of Emperor Claudius Caesar, a certain Simon, from Gitta in Samaria, practiced magic in both Samaria and Rome. It was there in Rome that Caesar gave Simon divine honors.[18] It is also said that Simon started a religious sect, called the *Simoniani,* which lasted well into the third century A.D.[19] Jerome quotes some Simonian writings where Simon claimed: "I am the word of God. I am the Comforter. I am the Almighty. I am all there is of God."[20] Clearly professions like these are an obvious attempt to corrupt orthodoxy by mixing occultism with fundamental tenets of Christian doctrine. *Clementine's Homilies and Recognitions* records that there were prolonged arguments between the Apostle Peter and Simon at both Antioch and Caesarea. Clementine reports that Peter spent much time undoing the havoc caused by Simonian heresy.[21]

If we attest to Solomon's proverbial wisdom, we understand that there is *nothing new under the sun*. Heretics such as Simon are not merely closet cultists with a few dimwit followers, but have contaminated a great many people with damnable heresies that have surfaced throughout the ages in one form or another. Without a doubt, Simon did considerable doctrinal damage by sowing discord amongst the young church for the first few centuries. Further historical evidence of this is documented in the following.

> Simon Magus, who unquestionably adulterated Christianity with pagan ideas and practices, and gave himself out, in pantheistic style, for an emanation of God. Plain traces of his error in the later epistles of Paul (to the Colossians, to Timothy, and to Titus), the second epistle of Peter, the first two epistles of John, the epistle

of Jude and messages of the Apocalypse. This heresy,
in the second century, spread over the whole church,
east and west in the various schools on Gnosticism.[22]

During the time the Church was still in its infancy, there were many
philosophies that contended with Christianity. One of the main groups
of heretics was the *Gnostics*. The word *Gnostic* means *relating to, or possess-
ing, intellectual or spiritual knowledge*.[23] Simon was a major proponent of
the Gnostic doctrine. Early Church fathers held that Gnosticism had
first-century roots and that Simon the Sorcerer of Samaria was the
first Gnostic.[24] The Gnostics placed heavy emphasis on the spirit. To
them all *matter* was declared as evil, but the spirit was the divine part of
man because it was *nonmaterial*. They claimed that their knowledge of
God was esoteric and spiritual.

To combat Gnosticism, John warned his readers to be rigidly discriminating concerning the *"spirit"* that moved a teacher in a church. The
fundamental test to apply to a teacher concerning his disposition to-
ward Christ was that if the teacher denied the *incarnation* or *bodily* resurrection of Christ, then he was to be rejected as a false teacher. John
declared that it was an *Anti-Christ* spirit that was operating through
those teachers. Remember, to the Gnostic, since only the spirit was
pure, Christ's incarnation and his bodily resurrection would not have
been acceptable to their idea of purity. Therefore, they espoused that
Christ could not have come in the flesh.

Another philosophy similar to Gnostic teaching was *Docetism*, which
was the very early heresy that taught that our blessed Lord had a body
like ours, but only in appearance, not in reality.[25] It is no wonder why
Jesus addressed this very issue when He appeared again to his disciples, knowing that His bodily resurrection would be challenged. He
told Thomas, "See my hands and my feet, that it is I myself. Touch
me, and see. For a spirit does not have flesh and bones as you see that
I have" (Luke 24:39, ESV). In his first epistle John states, "That which
was from the beginning, which we have heard, which we have seen

with our eyes, which we have looked upon, *and our hands have handled,* concerning the Word of life…"(1 John 1:1, NKJV). This simple yet powerful truth is a line of demarcation between truth and heresy, life and death. Without the bodily resurrection of Christ, Christianity collapses, and our faith is in vain.

The residual effect of Simon's heresy and the lasciviousness that it produced were seen centuries later in the Roman Catholic Church through an accepted practice called *Simony*. In Acts, Simon attempted to buy the Holy Spirit, giving way to the use of the term Simony (Acts 8:18). However, Simony took on a new meaning as men often bought their way into offices and political leadership within the church hierarchy, leading to much corruption.[26] There are also Gnostic gospels such as the *Gospel of Thomas,* discovered in Hammadi Egypt in 1945, which is full of heresy and goes as far as not supporting the resurrection of Christ.[27]

However, with all of his heresy and hocus-pocus, Simon's departure from this world was quite befitting. "According to *Hippolytus*, the earliest authority on the subject, Simon was buried alive at his own request, in the confident assurance that he would rise on the third day."[28] Well, one thing is for sure, we do not need verification from a credible historic source for us to know how that turned out! Though Simon did not rise from the dead, I do believe that just as depicted in Jesus' account of *Lazarus and the Rich Man,* "Simon lifted up his eyes in hell." It is amazing how one man can cause so much trouble, and it is why we must be on guard not to entertain deceivers. The Bible declares, "…if they speak not according to this word, *it is* because *there is* no light in them" (Isa.8:20).

One would think that in the 21st century we would be much further along. That with all our churches, and church organizations, and a Christian population that spans the globe, we would be fortified against the advent of false prophets. However, nothing could be further from the truth. The concerns that the apostle Paul had about the members of the church at Corinth who lived amongst well-entrenched pagan cults, mysticism, oracles, and false prophets still applies to us today. Here is what Paul says:

> But I am afraid that as the serpent deceived Eve by his cunning, your thoughts will be led astray from a sincere and pure devotion to Christ. For if someone comes and proclaims another Jesus than the one we proclaimed, or if you receive a different spirit from the one you received, or if you accept a different gospel from the one you accepted, you put up with it readily enough.
>
> 2 Corinthians 11:3-4, ESV

Though the apostle observed that the Corinthians were lacking in no spiritual gift (1 Cor. 1:7), yet this church had a lot of disorder going on. There were cliques, schisms, and rampant carnality. For this purpose, Paul had to set order in the church, something that *they were* lacking. Paul was concerned for the Corinthians because they could be easily duped. All someone had to do was come in with great oratorical skills, quote a few verses, show some signs and wonders, and they would be off to the races. This is a very sad commentary on the Corinthian church back then, and a reality and indictment for us today. There is nothing new under the sun.

Behold, I am against those who prophesy lying dreams, declares
the LORD, and who tell them and lead my people astray by
their lies and their recklessness, when I did not send them or
charge them. So they do not profit this people at all,
declares the LORD.
Jeremiah 23:32, ESV

CHAPTER 3

MANY FALSE PROPHETS
A SIGN OF THE END TIMES

At that time many will turn away from the faith and will betray and hate each other, and many false prophets will appear and deceive many people. For false messiahs and false prophets will appear and perform great signs and wonders to deceive, if possible, even the elect.
Matthew 24:4,10-11,24

On May 14th, 1948, Israel sent political shock waves around the world when it became a nation, after almost two-thousand years of not having a homeland. Since that momentous day, interest in end-time biblical prophecy has been consistently on the rise. Prophecy pundits from all over the world have scanned the horizon looking at places like the Middle East, the European Union, and Rome for the next event to be checked off the list of prophetic events. Though many of us today approach end-time prophecy with enthusiasm and interest, there were those in Jesus' day that were just as eager to know about the end-times. In Matthew 24, during Jesus' Mount Olivet discourse, the disciples asked the Lord the same question that many of us are still asking today, "When will these things be?"

Throughout the Mount Olivet discourse, Jesus listed several signs and events that will come upon the world just prior to His return. Things such as wars and rumors of war, famines, floods, pestilences, earthquakes in different places, and distress amongst the nations are just some of the many crises the world will face. In verse 8, Jesus referred to these as the "beginning of sorrows," or the *birth pangs*. This means that the duration between occurrences would decrease while the intensity of these events would increase, like a woman's pangs do as she approaches her delivery date. The famines, floods, and earthquakes are the signs that most prophecy students focus on, because they make sensational headlines. However, one of the most important end-time signs that will not move the Richter scale or hit the news cycles because it is a calamity of a spiritual nature—but that will affect churches around the world—is deception. It should be noted that before any mention of natural disasters or distress between nations, Jesus warns, "Take heed that no one deceives you..." (Matt. 24:4). Christ's first concern was that His followers not fall prey to deception from those who would attempt to predict the timing of His return. But I also believe this is an allusion to another form of deception here as well.

In the age of modern technology in which we now live, deception is running rampant. Deception is worldwide, from mass media where politicians and special-interest groups manipulate the masses through propaganda, subterfuge, and fake news to computer hackers stealing others' identities for financial gain. There is also deception when it comes to morality and sin, where the line between what's right and wrong is so blurred that it is hard to tell the difference between the two. Deception is pervasive. No segment of society is immune to its incursion.

In verse 5, Jesus emphasizes, "for many shall come in my name... and deceive many." It has always been Satan's agenda to usurp Christ and be worshiped as God. The first manifestation of that quest started with Eve in the Garden of Eden when the Devil questioned what God had said concerning the Tree of Knowledge. Since that terrible day when sin entered into the world, people have fallen victim to the schemes of Satan, who was a liar (deceiver) from the beginning (John 8:44).

> *False prophets need the right church environments in order to flourish. The question is, has your church created the environment to receive a false prophet?*

Satan's lies, his deceptions, his schemes are all promoted through the agenda of the kingdom of darkness in spiritual realms. The Devil utilizes ranks of demons that Paul identifies as the rulers, the authorities, the cosmic powers over this present darkness, the spiritual forces of evil in the heavenly places (Eph. 6:12, ESV). However, he also uses people to deceive and ultimately destroy other people. Among his most effective emissaries are a large number of false prophets, who lie in God's name to deceive and destroy as many people as he can, because Satan knows that he has but a short time.

Here is what the Lord says: "And many false prophets will arise and lead many astray (Matt.24:11, ESV). The word "many" comes from the Greek word *polys* [29] and is translated as *great, many, much,* and carries the idea of *plenteous* and *abundant.* From this we can see that in the last days, the world will be rife with these false prophets. False prophets can be found in many places throughout the world: prognosticators from occult religions, witch doctors, astrologers, palm readers, spirit guides, new age gurus, etc. There are countless false prophets who prey on individuals who are looking for someone to guide them through their affairs or to reveal what tomorrow holds. Even some banking and Wall Street executives have started consulting with Vedic astrologers to make predictions about market fluctuations. In a sense, all of these can be considered false prophets. But these are not the false prophets that pose the greatest threat to Christians. The false prophets that pose the greatest threat are the ones that operate within the Church.

One of the great questions concerning this reality is how is this possible? I believe the answer to this question is at least two-fold. In the second chapter, I examined Simon the Sorcerer, an individual back in the first century who wielded great influence over the people of Samaria through sorcery. I covered how Simon heard Philip the Evangelist's preaching and believed, was baptized, and then continued with Philip. Here is an example of how quickly wickedness can be introduced to a congregation. Everyone that is among the believers is not necessarily a true believer. Some, as Jesus warned, are wolves in sheep's clothing. This aspect I will cover in greater detail later. However, the second aspect that I feel is equally important to be examined is the fact that false prophets are readily finding an environment in which to operate. They are being welcomed and even encouraged to apply their deceptive trade in local churches, and even worse, among their followers on various social media platforms (online congregations) where there is absolutely no oversight or accountability.

CREATING THE ENVIRONMENT FOR FALSE PROPHETS

In order for any plant to grow, the conditions must be right. Every plant must have the right environment to thrive. For example, on Chicago's lakefront at Navy Pier, there are numerous palm trees! One might ask how a palm tree can survive the harsh conditions of a below-zero winter on Chicago's lakefront. Easily, at the Crystal Gardens, on Chicago's famed Navy Pier, the right environment has been created. This botanical garden is a six-story, climate-controlled glass structure, with a fifty-foot atrium, where over eighty palm trees and exotic plants flourish year-round. On the other hand, in Dubai tourists can go snow skiing on man-made indoor ski slopes in the middle of a sweltering desert, simply because the right environment has been created. When the right conditions exist, almost anything can flourish. The same is true for false prophets. False prophets need the right church environments in order to flourish. The question is, has your church created the environment to receive false prophecy?

In the book of Jeremiah, there are many warnings about false prophets and the destruction that they leave in their wake. However, this is a two-pronged problem, because false prophets are senders, but in order for them to function, they have to have willing receivers. In Jeremiah 29, here is what the Lord said about the false prophets:

> Yes, this is what the LORD Almighty, the God of Israel, says: "Do not let the prophets and diviners among you deceive you. Do not listen to the dreams you encourage them to have. They are prophesying lies to you in my name. I have not sent them," declares the LORD.
>
> Jeremiah 29:8-9

This passage is very informative, because it gives us insight into the environment the people created for false prophecy to be received. The Lord says, "Do not listen to the dreams *you* encourage them to have." In other words, it is the people's desire that is projected onto the false prophets, who in turn give back to the people a prophetic message that *they* want to hear. The people were the ones that created the demand for a false prophet to come and deceive them. This problem has been an ongoing issue since the beginning of time. It is a problem that transcends age, because it emanates from the heart. Therefore, the false prophets are reflections of a nation's or congregation's carnal desires. Placating sin-sick, wicked desires is the worst thing that can be done, because it encourages people to continue in their iniquity and not come to repentance. Introducing a prophet to that situation sends the wrong message, because it gives the impression that God is approving. The end result is that instead of getting better, the people get worse.

For example, if everyone in the congregation wants wealth and prosperity, because they attend a church that primarily teaches that the purpose for a relationship with God is so He can make you rich, then a false prophet can come to that church and prophesy about people becoming wealthy. That would be the message that this type of congregation would want to hear. In this example, the church's doctrine and the people's lust for wealth set the stage for a false prophet to exploit.

A true prophetic message that discloses the secrets of people's hearts would not be welcomed, but would be vehemently rejected. Many of today's prophets insist that a prophet should never call out someone's sin in front of the congregation. However, in response to that, I would refer them to the Scriptures (1 Cor. 14:24-25), where Paul suggests doing just that.

TELL US LIES

Here in Isaiah, we have a similar indictment. The prophet pulls no punches when he calls out the wickedness of God's people who desire a false prophet's message. Here is what the Lord says through Isaiah:

> Now go and write down these words. Write them in a book. They will stand until the end of time as a witness that these people are stubborn rebels who refuse to pay attention to the LORD's instructions. They tell the seers, "Stop seeing visions!" They tell the prophets, "Don't tell us what is right. Tell us nice things. Tell us lies. Forget all this gloom. Get off your narrow path. Stop telling us about your 'Holy One of Israel.'"
>
> Isaiah 30:8-11, NLT

This is disturbing on many levels. First of all, God instructed Isaiah not to speak this message, but He wanted Isaiah to "write it in a book" so the message would be an enduring witness, even until the end of time. This is important, because a verbal message can go in one ear and out the other. However, God wanted this message to be for all generations, because the dynamic between hard-hearted people and a false prophet was a concern for the people back then just as it is today. God wants people today to learn from people's mistakes of the past. Though circumstances may change, human nature doesn't. Therefore, "For whatsoever things were written aforetime were written for our learning, that we through patience and comfort of the Scriptures might have hope" (Rom.15:4, KJV).

> *The people were saying, we don't want to hear about the narrow path that leads to salvation...Tell us a soothing message of how loving God is, how He wants us all to be wealthy. We don't want to hear about God's holiness, nor his expectation for us to be holy.*

THE FOUR INDICTMENTS

In Isaiah's prophecy there are four serious indictments. The first one is *they are stubborn rebels*. The rebellious are people who not only refuse to conform but actively fight against any attempts to be conformed. Rebellion by nature is aggressive, not passive. In a rebellion, people don't just complain, they vent their anger in riotous action. From God's viewpoint, rebellion is synonymous with the sin of witchcraft, because obstinate resistance exalts self-will to the place of authority, which belongs only to God. Therefore, it is as bad as witchcraft, and tantamount to *idolatry*, because the self has usurped God's place.[30]

Secondly, *they refused to receive instruction from the Lord*. They refused to hear the words of the prophet. A graphic illustration of this comes to mind where in the book of Acts, right before they stoned Stephen,"…they covered their ears and, yelling at the top of their voices, they all rushed at him, dragged him out of the city and began to stone him…" (Acts 7:57-58). Stephen gave a retrospective assessment of Israel's rebellious history which so angered the Pharisees that they refused to hear anymore from him. They literally covered their ears and then brutally stoned him to death. Why? Because a rebellious people do not want to be told the truth, even if the truth is coming from God, whom they claim to be serving. In John 15:5, Jesus said, "Without me you can do nothing."All things come from God, and we are complete in Him. How is it, then, that people do not want to know about God, from whom all blessings flow? How is it that our affections have turned from God, so that we would rather learn of another way? In ancient

Israel, this rebellious people had turned to serving other gods and was now rejecting the only one and true God.

The third indictment is that they *rejected God's messenger and tried to temper his message.* "They tell the seers, 'Stop seeing visions!' They tell the prophets, 'Don't tell us what is right. Tell us nice things. Tell us lies. Forget all this gloom.'" In essence, this is what the people were saying: stop telling us the truth; we don't want to hear about our backsliding, we don't want to hear about our sin, we don't want to know about what God's heart is about how we are living. Just tell us nice things. Lie to us about us becoming rich and how we will have no more difficulties. As long as the message is not offensive and you are not convicting us about our iniquity, a lying prophecy will do just fine! The message of a false prophet will always be a nice, sweet message primarily directed towards things that gratify the lust of the flesh.

The fourth indictment is *Get off your narrow path. Stop telling us about your "Holy One of Israel."* Once again, what the people were saying was, we don't want to hear about the narrow path that leads to salvation. Show us the broad path, even if it leads us to destruction. We just want to eat, drink, and be merry; we are not interested in all the doom and gloom things about God being a *consuming fire*, or about how it is a *fearful thing to fall into the hands of the living God.* No, tell us a soothing message of how loving God is, how He wants us all to be wealthy. We don't want to hear about God's holiness, nor his expectation for us to be holy. We don't want to learn about God's righteousness given to us in His holy Word. Besides, that's old and outdated; no one lives like that today anyway.

This is heartbreaking. How could God's people be so callous back then, and how can they be even more callous today? Again, in order for a false prophet to thrive, there must be an environment created for him. So from this standpoint, it is not just the false prophets to be blamed here, but it is the people who encourage the false prophets to lie, deceive, and have false dreams.

> *False prophets will claim that they have seen Jesus, or that they communicate with angels, or that signs and wonders follow their ministry...of course none that are verifiable.*
>
>

THAT WAS THEN, THIS IS NOW?

There are those of you reading this book that may feel this was an Old Testament problem. They may muse: people today do not act this way towards God or His ministers. We are on the other side of the Cross. We have Christ within us. We have a completed Bible. We have the Holy Spirit, and great churches and authentic dedicated and anointed pastors. However, this is not just an Old Testament phenomenon, but has transcended the ages and is found in churches today. In 2 Timothy, Paul gives this solemn warning:

> For the time is coming when [people] will not tolerate (endure) sound *and* wholesome instruction, but, having ears itching [for something pleasing and gratifying], they will gather to themselves one teacher after another to a considerable number, chosen to satisfy their own liking *and* to foster the errors they hold.
>
> 2 Timothy 4:3, AMP

The similarities between Isaiah 30:8-11 and 2 Timothy 4:3 are striking. Paul warns that the time was coming when he says "...when [people] will not tolerate (endure) sound *and* wholesome instruction...." This directly corresponds with Isaiah 30, "...stubborn rebels who refuse to pay attention to the LORD's instructions." Secondly, Paul asserts "... having ears itching [for something pleasing and gratifying], they will gather to themselves one teacher after another..." This corresponds to Isaiah's prophecy, "...tell the prophets, 'Don't tell us what is right. Tell us nice things. Tell us lies…'" I submit to you that these warnings are remarkably similar because the people are remarkably similar. To put it into today's vernacular, "They ain't changed a bit!"

It is important to note that the apostle emphasizes that "the time will come," meaning that whenever the opportunity presents itself, be it near or distant future, this rebellious attitude amongst believers will be prevalent. The reason for this is that wherever there is a lack of attention to sound doctrine, the people will suffer from spiritual malnutrition from being fed a junk-food doctrinal diet. Under these circumstances, going to church simply becomes a perfunctory activity where people congregate to sing, praise, and pray without any substantive attention given to the word of God. Sunday is not the time where in-depth study of the Word occurs. Normally, in-depth study occurs during the mid-week Bible class or through other weekly educational programs where members can gain an increased knowledge of biblical exposition and doctrine. The problem is that only a fraction of those that attend Sunday worship services attend mid-week Bible class to further their biblical literacy in any meaningful way. The congregation normally reflects the spirit of their pastor. If the pastor is loose, then more likely the congregation will be loose. If the pastor doesn't promote sound doctrine, then the congregates will not place importance on fidelity to the Scripture as a priority.

In 2 Timothy 4:3, Paul indicates that the people would seek out *teachers* as opposed to *prophets*. Therefore, some would argue that this passage is not speaking specifically of false prophets, but of corrupt teachers. However, that line of reasoning is problematic, because prophets also function as teachers and preachers and vice-versa. In the following text, false prophets that teach are identified. "The elders and dignitaries are the head, the *prophets who teach lies* are the tail" (Isa.9:15). But also in the New Testament the Word of God teaches:

> But there were also false prophets in Israel, just as there
> will be false teachers among you. They will cleverly

teach destructive heresies and even deny the Master who bought them. In this way, they will bring sudden destruction on themselves. Many will follow their evil teaching and shameful immorality. And because of these teachers, the way of truth will be slandered. In their greed they will make up clever lies to get hold of your money. But God condemned them long ago, and their destruction will not be delayed.

2 Peter 2:1-3, NLT

Once again, there is clear harmony in the Scriptures. Peter draws a parallel between New Testament false teachers and Old Testament false prophets, referring to their teachings as *destructive* (NIV) or *damnable* (KJV) heresies. Of these false teachers *The Tyndale Commentary* observes that "their teaching was flattery; their ambitions were financial; their lives were dissolute; their conscience was dulled, and their aim was deception."[31] In the NIV, verse 3 reads as follows, "In their greed these teachers will exploit you with fabricated stories." The first of eight ways to recognize a false prophet (that I will be covering later) is that they must convince you that they are God's anointed prophet by lying to build their credibility. They do that so you will not only obey them but fear them as well. Fear them, meaning you won't challenge their authority.

Many of these false prophets will say that they have seen Jesus, or that Jesus appeared to them in a dream and gave them special revelations, or that they commune with angels, or that signs and wonder follow their ministry (of course none that are verifiable), or that they talk with Jesus regularly. However, the real motivating factor behind all of this is so they can raise hefty offerings. This is what Peter is saying in verse 3, "In their greed these teachers (false prophets) will exploit you with fabricated stories…" False prophets will always tell you what great exploits they have done. It is important for them to get you to buy in to their brand. They do this to win your confidence. Once they have your confidence, they can get your money.

IT'S ALL ABOUT THE MONEY

The *New Living Translation* really emphasizes this in verse 3, where it reads, "In their greed they will make up clever lies to get hold of your money." Once I was talking to a person who visited a certain church in the Midwest. She spoke of how anointed the services were because there was a powerful prophet there who was "very accurate." She then said that after he preached and prophesied to many people, it was then offering time. The prophet started encouraging people to "sow a seed"*(which means give your money)*. He then prophesied, and said that those who gave would receive one-hundred-fold in return. People hurried to give, so he had people lining up in different money lines, a $50 line, a $100 line, even a $1,000 line. She was amazed that not only did people get in the $50 and $100 lines, but several people got in the $1,000 line too. Of course, if you didn't have cash, they would accept credit and debit cards.

After the offering is collected and tallied, the prophet receives a hefty share of the offering raised. Sometimes there are two offerings raised, where the church gets the proceeds of the first offering, and the prophet gets to keep all of the offering he raises. If they do not reach a certain amount of money, they have more offerings. One eyewitness that used to attend a scamming church said that in order to encourage the people to give, certain members would give fifty and one-hundred dollars just to get others to give the same. But, after the service, they would go and get their money back!

Years ago I attended a conference where a prophet was raising an offering. People felt compelled, some maybe even intimidated, because he yelled and screamed at the people through the blaring P.A. system. It was reminiscent of the *Wizard of Oz*, where the wizard was terrifying Dorothy, the tin man, the lion, and the scarecrow while hiding behind a curtain and yelling into a microphone. There was an elderly lady who had $20 in her hand. She didn't want to give the whole twenty, but wanted change back. This prophet stood in front of this woman, yelling at the top of his lungs into the microphone for this lady "to loose" that twenty-dollars, making her feel guilty about not giving to God. The poor woman held on to her money as long as she could, but he practically snatched it out of her hands. It was outrageous but unfortunately not unusual.

The exploitation of God's people for money has always been a problem. When the apostle Paul gave his final words to those in Miletus as he prepared to depart for Jerusalem, here is what he said:

> So guard yourselves and God's people. Feed and shepherd God's flock—his church, purchased with his own blood—over which the Holy Spirit has appointed you as elders. I know that false teachers, like vicious wolves, will come in among you after I leave, not sparing the flock. Even some men from your own group will rise up and distort the truth in order to draw a following.
>
> Acts 20:28-30, NLT

> I have never coveted anyone's silver or gold or fine clothes. You know that these hands of mine have worked to supply my own needs and even the needs of those who were with me. And I have been a constant example of how you can help those in need by working hard. You should remember the words of the Lord Jesus: 'It is more blessed to give than to receive.'
>
> Acts 20:33-35, NLT

Paul's departing words of admonition to the saints at Miletus and those who had come from Ephesus were filled with compassion and emotion. His departing words were most telling. These final words were not only advice, but a solemn charge to these beloved saints, because Paul knew that he would never see their faces again. I stress this point, because this was Paul's last chance to reiterate with strong emphasis for what these brothers should prepare.

The first charge was to *"guard yourselves and God's people."* This charge reflects the vigilance of a pastor's heart and commitment to guard and protect the flock at all costs. As under shepherds, the care and nurturing of God's people is a serious issue, because they must give an account for the people's souls. "Guard yourselves," Paul charged, against the false prophets and teachers, those ravenous wolves that are sure to come. Their damnable doctrines are often sweet to the taste but deadly if swallowed.

In this case, Paul said that these teachers would manifest "as soon as I leave." Paul then said, *"And men will rise up from your own number with deviant doctrines to lure the disciples into following them…"* (Acts 20:30, HCSB). Paul knew that these false prophets were already among "their own number," looking to subvert and convert proselytes to themselves upon Paul's departure. Paul understood what was really at stake, because anyone who does follow their pernicious heresies is surely headed for destruction. Although these prophets feed their massive egos by those who follow them, the main reason they want followers is so they can get their money.

In today's social media-crazed world, two words have taken on a whole new meaning, *followers* and *friends,* meaning people that you have never met being your friends, and people that you have not met personally following you. On social media, people can portray an alternate personality simply for the purpose of getting a following and amassing friends. Some internet stars have thousands and even millions of followers, without leaving their residences. False prophets typically exploit this as a way of directly marketing their pernicious brand to others. Though false prophets are not the only ones that have big online followings, it gives them access to people's lives and eventually their pocketbooks, where they can practice divination while calling it prophecy. Just a note of clarity: there are many good ministries that also have a commanding presence on the internet and social media. Remember, my study is about "false prophets."

I once saw two very well-known prosperity preachers running and shuffling their feet over an altar full of money. They literally looked like fools as they yelled out "want your bills paid!" The congregation went berserk, and even more of them started running to the altar to bring more money so the minster could dance on top of it, exclaiming, "I'm anointing this money." It brought tears to my eyes as I witnessed the grace of God being turned into lasciviousness.

Paul's second charge was "…I have never coveted anyone's silver or gold or fine clothes." Paul said he was never after anyone else's money! Not so with false prophets; they by nature are covetous, wanting other people's money transferred to them. However, Paul's life and ministry were an example of self-sacrifice, not self-exaltation as you see false prophets doing. Paul stated that he worked with his own hands to provide for the necessities of himself and those with him. There was no *"lifestyles of the rich and famous"* with Paul.

Then his closing charge was, "You should remember the words of the Lord Jesus: 'It is more blessed to give than to receive.'" Although this statement is not found explicitly in the Gospel narratives, the concept is certainly taught. In the teaching of Jesus, generosity to others is an antidote to covetousness and a way to escape the captivating deceit of riches.[32] However, you never see the false prophets sowing their seed to the poor. It's always one way. When you sow to them, it's always, "God will bless you," not them! If they really believed what Paul said—"It is more blessed to give than to receive"—then they should be the biggest givers, not the biggest takers! If they really believed in sowing a seed for harvest and increase, then they would bring money to a service and distribute their money to the people, so God in turn would bless them with an increase. Do not the Scriptures declare that "God loves a cheerful giver"(2 Cor. 9:7)?

In Luke 18:22, we find Jesus' encounter with the rich young ruler, where Jesus tells him to "sell all that you have, give it to the poor, you will have treasure in heaven...." This formula (sell what you have, give it to the poor, receive treasure in heaven) would never work for a false prophet, because they wouldn't give their money to the poor. They want the poor or anyone else to give their money to them! Secondly, they would never give away their money and possessions in exchange for treasures in heaven. They don't want pie in the sky. They want their dough down here on the ground!

CHAPTER 4

ACTS OF THE FALSE PROPHETS

Speaking of false prophets, Jesus stated, "Ye shall know them by their fruits..."(Matt.7:15-16). Therefore, knowing the acts or methods of the false prophets is very important for discerning some of the pervasive deception occurring in churches and social media platforms around the world. On any given day, a so-called prophet, prophetess, pastor, apostle, or whatever title they choose, will walk into a church, preach a message, and then start prophesying some vague, nonsensical, nonspecific mumbo-jumbo that sounds deep but is void of substance. After hyping and wowing those people the "prophets" have primed for pumping, the people are then fleeced with the *sow a seed* con game, through one or more offerings. Many false prophets keep the offering going until they reach a certain amount.

In Micah 3:11, God calls out the acts of the false prophets when he says: "...her prophets tell fortunes for money. Yet they look for the LORD's support and say, 'Is not the LORD among us....'" In this passage God is uncovering these false prophets as mere fortunetellers! But even more scandalous, they claim they have the Lord's backing and approval by saying, "Is not the LORD among us?" False prophets always tout that the presence of the Lord is in the room, because they must have some sort of validation in order to prep the people to give their money. Before we delve further into this subject matter, I would like to share a few incidents that will punctuate the premise of this chapter.

> *The people said Simon the sorcerer was "the great power of God." This has always been a big problem, because people have the tendency to associate anything supernatural with God. But all things supernatural are not all things Godly.*

THE NAME AND NUMBERS GAME

Not long ago, I had a conversation with an associate who attended a Pentecostal worship service in Chicago. They were excited to report to me how God showed up in a mighty way through signs and wonders manifested during this service. Here is the essence of what they said:

> "This young prophet had a heavy anointing. He was so accurate. He could walk down the aisles and was calling out some people's names and other's addresses, even some Social Security numbers. People were amazed at how God was really using him!"

In chapter one, *The Message of a Prophet*, I covered that a true prophet is God's mouthpiece. Therefore, the prophet of the Lord receives a message from an all-knowing God that sees and knows everything. The Lord's primary objective when giving a prophetic message is not to appease or entertain people, but is to reveal His truth and righteousness in the earth realm according to God's purposes and plans. It's not about revealing some irrelevant fact about an individual in order to impress the recipient or the audience. This is the type of thing you would see at a carnival, magic show, or on some psychic network.

My associate's statement above is exactly what the people said about Simon the sorcerer, that he was "the great power of God." This has always been a big problem, because people have the tendency to associate anything supernatural with God. But as we stated earlier, "All things supernatural are not all things Godly." Demons are supernatural! Sorcery is supernatural because by definition it means "the use of supernatural power over others through the assistance of spirits." However, in this case, the prophet was able to discern names and numbers of those that they chose to call out for a prophecy.

One of the biggest schemes that false prophets (or any false ministers) use is the name and numbers game. It is particularly effective in settings where the right environment is set for false prophecy to operate. In Isaiah, here is what a rebellious generation wanted from the prophets. "They tell the seers, 'Stop seeing visions!' They tell the prophets, 'Don't tell us what is right. Tell us nice things. Tell us lies.'"(Isa.30:9-10, NLT) As we have covered previously, false prophecy has two legs, a prophet willing to lie, and people that want to be lied to. People who want to be lied to are not seeking sound doctrine, because they have itching ears for "signs and wonders" and the "supernatural manifestations." They willingly reject sound teaching so they can satisfy the lust of their flesh. They constantly seek their next fix of supernatural impartation so they can partake in what they call the deep things of God to gratify their covetousness. This is why if a prophet tells them their name or number, they see that as God revealing this to the prophet, but this is simply nothing more than fortunetelling. People do not want to hear redeeming truth but would rather hear "nice things."

In Micah 3:11, we see that *fortunetelling* is a centuries-old form of divination that has lured and deceived people since the times before recorded history. Micah says, "and her prophets tell fortunes for money. Yet they look for the LORD's support and say, 'Is not the LORD among us...'" Here is the question, if God were going to send a prophet to the people that live in the midst of a crooked and perverse generation, filled with people that have all sorts of issues and iniquity within their heart, why would God have a prophet tell people their name or phone number? People already know their contact information! Would not God show His righteousness by revealing people's sins so they could repent, be reconciled, and subsequently be blessed to avoid the consequences of unrighteousness? Or warn them from some impending danger? Or reveal specifics about His plan for their lives? Remember what God said through Jeremiah in Lamentations:

> Your prophets saw misleading visions about you. They painted a good picture of you. They didn't expose your guilt in order to make things better again. They gave you false prophecies that misled you.
>
> Lamentations 2:14, GW

In chapter two we covered the concept of creating the environment for false prophecy to exist. In a healthy church that teaches sound doctrine, you will not find a false prophet operating. Christians that are taught sound doctrine will not be out looking for someone to give them "a Word." But the characteristics of those who are positioned to be deceived are found in 2 Timothy 3:

> They will act religious, but they will reject the power that could make them godly. Stay away from people like that! They are the kind who work their way into people's homes and win the confidence of vulnerable women who are burdened with the guilt of sin and controlled by various desires. (Such women are forever following new teachings, but they are never able to understand the truth.)
>
> 2 Timothy 3:5-7, NLT

The reason why people who are burdened with guilt and sin are seeking out new teachings and even a "word from the Lord" is because of sin. They cannot hear from God for themselves. People who are in bondage to sin want someone to tell them nice things. This is the psychological profile of someone who is ripe to be deceived. These unstable souls can never come to the knowledge of the truth, because they are receiving lies from false prophets and teachers. This is how the environment is created for the false prophet. These same silly women and men that have no sound doctrinal roots are easily moved and impressed with foolish antics like someone calling out their name or phone number. Despite the fact that in this day and age that we live, there are a hundred ways someone can find out your personal information over the internet. But instead of being sober-minded and vigilant, like the Samaritans in Acts 8, they too would proclaim, "This is the power of God."

For a note of clarity, false prophecy is not limited to just those that carry the title prophet. *Anyone* who gives prophecy to an individual or stands before the people in person or through social media, or by whatever means, and gives "a prophetic word," no matter what their actual title may be, whether it's apostle, pastor, teacher, evangelist, brother, sister, deacon, whatever the title, can be a channel of false prophecy and therefore a false prophet. However, for the sake of clarity, I will keep this study focused upon those who carry the title "prophet," but this deception is not at all restricted to a specific title or office.

EXHIBIT A: A FALSE PROPHET IN ACTION

One of the biggest mysteries concerning false prophets is how do they do it? How are they able to know information about complete strangers? The assumption is, God must be speaking to them, right? Wrong! That's exactly what they want you to think.

The following dialog was taken from a YouTube video of a prophet in action. Step by step, we will analyze this trickster's methods. I am not concerned with identifying who this prophet is, but more importantly, we want to examine this false prophet's methods.

In the first directive, the false prophet says,

"Everybody lift up their hands."

Those of us that attend Pentecostal churches are used to raising our hands, because it symbolizes reverence and submission to God. However, when a false prophet does it, he wants the submission to be to him or her, because at that point they are directing the flow of the service and need you to be submissive to them. This has nothing to do with worshiping the Lord in spirit and truth, because they're in the process of setting people up. There is nowhere in the Scriptures where Jesus told anyone to raise their hands before he performed a miracle. Nor did the apostles or the prophets of old use this technique. This is used to bring people under the power of the prophet's suggestion. To be clear, I am not saying that during corporate or individual worship no one should ever raise their hands; *this is* clearly biblical (Ps. 142:2). However, by nature, a false prophet cannot invoke the presence of God, therefore when they do it, it's manipulation.

Next the prophet says,

"I have come to deliver a rhema word to let you know that the struggle is over."

As Pentecostals and Charismatics use it, a *rhema* [33] word is that which is spoken by God to an individual. The problem with so-called rhema words is they are subjective and cannot be substantiated by anyone else. Rhema words such as "Your struggles are over" is another one of these nonsensical, subjective statements. No matter how godly you are, you will always have struggles in this life. Don't let anyone tell you anything different. The only people whose struggles are over in this life are those who are dead. Everyone else—rich, poor, free, and bond—will have their portion of struggles. Even the Lord had struggles. In Acts 14:22, here is what the Scriptures say about the struggles in this life of a believer: "Strengthening the disciples and encouraging them to remain true to the faith. We must go through many hardships to enter the kingdom of God..." (Acts 14:22; also see John 16:33, 1 Thes. 3:3, 2 Tim. 3:12).

After this false prophet lies to the people about their struggles being over, he then prophesies,

"I hear the Lord saying that he is going to birth multimillionaires… God is going to cause the economy of your life to shift, because the wealth of the wicked is stored up for the saints."

He's a liar. The Lord hasn't told him anything. Messages like this are designed to get greedy and gullible people primed to give in the offering. False prophets usually connect the promised manifestation of wealth in people's lives to the proportion that they give in the offering. Using the ministry for financial gain has been around for thousands of years. This is why the Scriptures say, "…and her prophets tell fortunes for money" (Micah 3:11). The prophet then goes on to say,

"…the wealth of the wicked is stored up for the saints. No good thing will he withhold from you."

Here, the false prophet is connecting two passages of Scripture (Prov. 13:22 and Ps. 84:11) to create the delusion of imminent wealth to be released upon the people in the room. This is what the Scriptures call *handling the Word of God deceitfully*. In response to this, let me connect two Scriptures as well: "Cursed *be* he that doeth the work of the LORD deceitfully…," (Jer.48:10, KJV) and, secondly, "Rather, we have renounced secret and shameful ways; we do not use deception, nor do we distort the word of God. On the contrary, by setting forth the truth plainly, we commend ourselves to everyone's conscience in the sight of God" (2 Cor.4:2).

Again, the false prophet then commands,

"…lift up those hands tonight as a sign of surrender."

Again, neither Jesus nor the prophets ever told anyone to lift up their hands as a sign of surrender before they prophesied to them or performed a miracle. However, this command forces the question, surrender to whom? This is a control-and-manipulation technique used to bring people under the influence of the prophet's suggestion. Then the false prophet goes to the next level by proclaiming,

"The presence of the Lord is here."

This is exactly what the Scriptures say false prophets do: "and her prophets tell fortunes for money. Yet they look for the LORD's support and say, 'Is not the LORD among us'" (Micah 3:11). In order to keep people adherent and submissive, the false prophet must reiterate that "God is here." The false prophet then proclaims,

"Everyone that wants something new in their life to come to the altar."

Again, he continues to issue commands to maintain control. He then says,

"I'm not a soothsayer or a psychic. I don't play with my gift."

Here the prophet is claiming legitimacy by stating that he *is not* a soothsayer or psychic. It's like the liar who swears they are telling the truth, before anyone accuses them of lying. It amounts to a subconscious admission. He's really defending against the conviction of his own conscience. After telling people to come to the altar, but they aren't coming quickly enough, he further commands,

"Y'all need to move! Man of God, come on up here. I got a prophetic word for you tonight."

Again, the false prophet continues his control. He then says,

"I didn't come here because I needed to preach. I came here because you need a word."

Here the false prophet uses another technique by making the people feel some obligation to come up to receive prophecy because he made "the sacrifice" to come there, and that they're the ones who need a word, not him. Then the prophet starts speaking in tongues, and looking up like he's receiving something directly from heaven. Then he says,

"I see angels all around the room."

Again, this is another manipulation technique, to make people think that he is on a higher level of spirituality than the rest, because *he can see the angels.* Compare this statement to Daniel's encounter with an angel. Daniel stated this angel had eyes as a flame of fire and a face that looked like lightning, and his words sounded like a multitude. This encounter caused Daniel so much trauma that it overwhelmed him and he passed out. After the angel revived him, Daniel said, "I stood trembling" (Dan. 10:4-12). Had an angel like this been in that room with the false prophet, people would have killed themselves trying to get out that door. If they don't appear in human form, angels are way beyond a human's ability to comprehend and could literally scare you to death. No doubt, all believers have angels assigned to them, but it's highly doubtful that he could see them.

Then the false prophet starts prophesying to an apostle that is in the service. He then says,

"The West Coast is going to come open to you. Virginia is going to come open too. I see another church opening up too."

The manipulation continues, because by prophesying to a ranking minister first (an apostle), all the rest of those there wouldn't dare challenge the false prophet's authority and would be anxious for him to give them a word too. The false prophet then says,

"I have not talked to this man. I do not believe in this new age where you go and search people out to get information. That's what some of these false prophets are doing!"

Again, defending his legitimacy when no one has challenged him is a dead giveaway. This false prophet is actually telling how some of *the other* false prophets operate, but of course, not him.

Then he tells the story of how he was in an accident and was ejected from the car. As his mother sat in the hospital room with him, she told him that when she was pregnant with him, the Angel of the Lord appeared to her and said,

"Your son (speaking of him) was going to be a prophet to the nations, that he would know dates and times and conditions in people's bodies."

First, in the Old Testament, "Angel of the Lord" is normally used as a deity in angelic form.[34] In other words, God in angelic form, i.e., the burning bush in Exodus, and it was the Angel of the Lord that Jacob wrestled with, where Jacob declared, "I have seen God face to face" (Ex. 3:6, Gen. 32:24-30). So what the false prophet is suggesting is that while he was in his mother's womb, an angel appeared to his mother and said her son would be a "prophet to the nations." It is doubtful whether this prophet prophesies to any nations or stands before high-ranking political figures to speak to them on behalf of God to a whole nation like Moses, Isaiah, Jeremiah, and Daniel did.

But then the prophet says something very interesting, stating,

"The angel of the Lord, said that he would know dates, times, and names, and conditions in people's bodies."

This is interesting because he reveals the parameters of his prophetic ability. Once again, no mention of revealing God's word, nothing about the righteousness or kingdom of God. He says nothing about God's plan for the nations, nothing about people being delivered from sin, nothing about the edification, comfort, or exhortation of the Church. If he is a prophet to the nations, then why would he only know "dates, times, and names, and conditions in people's bodies?" I will come back to this point later. After saying that, the false prophet goes on to prophesy to the apostle again, saying,

"I see a house of restoration, where you are going to be helping people that come out of jail. He said, 'You have many things written down that have not come to pass yet.'"

Once again, nonspecific rambling that could fit anyone's circumstances. How many people have ideas written down? Most pastors write down their ideas, even if it's only the sermon or Bible class notes. All churches should be places of restoration, and most churches have members that have been to jail at one time or another.

The most interesting part of this whole prophetic service is when the false prophet approaches a man in the service that isn't buying what this prophet is selling. Right before he approaches this person, the false prophet states,

"Some of you have been contaminated because a prophet has spoken a wrong word to you."

Again, all of this is just the setup for the prophet to start calling out people for a personal prophecy. Then he points out a man in this small audience of mostly women (which is typically the case in these settings, i.e., "silly women"). The prophet then says,

"Man in the front row. I see something in the spirit."

Then he says,

"Lift your hands."

If the prophet already sees something in the spirit about this man, then why does he insist that he lift his hands? What the false prophet is doing is gauging how submissive this man is going to be. Evidently, the man does not want to lift his hands, so the false prophet approaches closer and speaks in tongues briefly, then says,

"I hear the Lord saying, I'm getting ready to shift some things for you. Do you hear me tonight?"

Again, this is ridiculous. He hasn't heard the Lord saying anything. Besides, the Lord doesn't have to "get ready" to do anything. And shift what things? Deceivers talk like that, not God. First the false prophet says, "I'm seeing something in the spirit," but as soon as he detects hesitancy in the man, he switches to a more authoritative position now to be claiming to hear what the Lord Himself is saying. Then again, he asks,

"Can you lift your hands towards heaven? Are you able to lift them?"

Why is this false prophet so insistent that this man raise his hands? Particularly now that the prophet is standing right in front of him. Then the man asks him, "I want to know what the Lord is telling you." The false prophet immediately responds,

"What does the number 5252 mean to you… I don't know what it means, is it a road…what does it mean to you?"

The man replies,

"It's an address I am familiar with."

The prophet then responds,

The Lord has given this to you as a sign tonight that there is some unbelief in your spirit because of some hurt that you have been through. You have gone through some things where some people let you down. But as I am operating in word of knowledge tonight, the Lord said that this is the hour of your visitation. You're going to have to obey God. If not, there shall be a condition that begins to form in your body."

As soon as the false prophet says this, you can hear a woman's voice saying "Wow." Obviously this little showdown has impressed her. As for the man, he rebukes the false prophet and calls him out as operating in a spirit of divination. After which the false prophet insists that the man be removed from the church, shouting to the pastor, "Remove this man from the church!" The man starts quoting a Scripture from Jeremiah about false prophets. But the false prophet begins shouting the man down through the microphone, shouting out, "Satan, the Lord rebuke you." Then the false prophet says,

"There is a flow going on right now, and we must minister to the other people." What malarkey!

What we have just covered, though unbelievable, is not actually that unusual. Games like these are played in churches all over the world, particularly in America and even more so in Africa. In the next chapter, we will examine how the practice of divination is being passed off as prophecy.

Dear friends, do not believe everyone who claims to speak
by the Spirit. You must test them to see if the spirit they have
comes from God. For there are many false
prophets in the world.
1 John 4:1, NLT

CHAPTER FIVE

PROPHECY OR DIVINATION?

*Their visions are false and their divinations a lie. Even though the LORD
has not sent them, they say, "The LORD declares," and expect him to
fulfill their words. Have you not seen false visions and uttered
lying divinations when you say, "The LORD declares,"
though I have not spoken?*
Ezekiel 13:6-7

In the last chapter we analyzed the statements of a false prophet
and uncovered some of the chicanery that occurs in numerous
churches all over America. In that example, the false prophet
put much emphasis on people raising their hands. This leads to a point
in our study where we examine the art of Divination. *Divination* is the
practice of consulting beings, whether spiritual, human, or departed,
by the observation of objects or actions of things in an attempt to gain
information about the future and such matters as are removed from
normal knowledge. Divination is related to magic but is distinct from
it mainly in that the latter attempts to produce a certain effect, while
the former seeks knowledge.[35] Divination is used in Scriptures of *false*
systems of ascertaining the divine will. It has been universal in all ages
and all nations alike, civilized and savage.[36]

As Ezekiel states in chapter 13, verses 6-7, false prophets use divination. No matter how many Scriptures they quote or how often they
call the name of Jesus, they are not sent by God. They are deceivers.

The word *divination* is found fourteen times, *diviners* eleven times, and
divines seven times in the Scriptures. These references are primarily

found in the Old Testament, with only one occurrence in the New Testament (Acts 16:16). There are clear prohibitions against using any form of divination. Though there is not an explicit prohibition against the most popularized version of divination astrology, which is found in daily newspapers and online content all over America and throughout the world, it still falls under the general heading of divination (See Ex. 22:18; Lev. 19:26, 31; Lev. 20:27; Deut. 18:10, 11). Though some forms of divination like numerology and astrology are systems that chart one's character, other forms of divination such as sorcery, necromancy, and predicting the future require direct contact with demonic influence. However, even the more benign forms of divination (i.e., astrology) are gateways into the occult and demonic.

PALMISTRY

Palmistry is the art of predicting one's future and characteristics about a person's life based upon the lines on the palm of the hands, the shape of the hand, and the characteristics of the fingers. A reasonably skilled palm reader can take a cursory look at someone's hands and call out characteristics about their life, without having ever met them.

Those who are skilled in these forms of divination can walk into a room and read characteristics from a person's palms. One may ask, how does one read your palms while in church? Simple, the false prophet usually approaches the people they are going to prophesy to, coming within close proximity. They tell the individuals to raise their hands as a sign of worship or surrender. While the hands are raised, palms can be read. Again, this is a *possible* explanation of how a false prophet skilled in this form of divination can know personal characteristics about strangers. Am I suggesting that all false prophets operating in churches are palm readers too? No, I am not. However, I am saying that palm reading is a form of divination that is rampant in many countries around the world where divination is commonly practiced, of which America is one. Remember, it is the Lord that states false prophets use divination (Deut. 18:9-13).

FACE READING

The art of *face reading* also gives a person who practices divination a leg up on discerning characteristics of a complete stranger. Each one of us reads people's faces every day. We can look at a person's expression and detect what they might be thinking. However, in divination, face reading starts by looking at the shape of the face. For example, a person with an oval face with wide cheekbones, clear eyes, pale eyebrows, and a pale complexion, would be categorized as a *metal face,* which means that this person has a great sense of humor, is sensitive, and tends to be creative.[37] Several other aspects about the face, such as the eyes, eyebrows, the nose, mouth, ears, and where moles are on the face and rest of the body can give information about the person's character and future.

NUMEROLOGY

Another form of divination is *numerology*. The art of *numerology* identifies characteristics of a person through use of numbers. According to the *Fortune-Teller's Bible, A Definitive Guide to the Arts of Divination*, the numerological value of someone's name and date of birth reveals valuable information about a person's character.[38] A person's name can be divided into three categories to understand certain facets of their character.[39] Each letter of a person's name is assigned a numerical value and added up, along with the person's birth date. All these numbers are then matched to a *personality, heart, expression*, and *destiny* number.[40] These calculations allow one to do a reading on a person based on their name and birth date, without ever having met them!

All a false prophet needs is your name and birth date (more on this later). With palmistry, all a person needs to do is see your palms, and with a face reader, your character and fortune are written all over your face. This is why people that practice divination can only tell you *certain* things. These types of readings do not lend themselves to great detail or specifics.

Remember in the previous chapter the false prophet mentioned that he would know "dates, times, and names, and conditions in people's bodies." These are exactly what individuals that practice divination focus on. Let's start with "dates and times," and hear what the Lord said:

> There shall not be found among you *any one* that maketh his son or his daughter to pass through the fire, *or* **that useth divination, or an observer of times,** or an enchanter, or a witch, Or a charmer, or a consulter with familiar spirits, or a wizard, or a necromancer. For all that do these things *are* an abomination unto the LORD: and because of these abominations the LORD thy God doth drive them out from before thee.
>
> Deuteronomy 18:10-12, KJV

Verse 10 speaks specifically about the "observer of times" as being a part of *divination* that the Bible clearly forbids God's people to be involved in. There are other common methods of divination, the following being just a few.

Chresmology is the practice where predictions through oracles such as seers or prophets occur.[41] Chresmology would be the divination counterpart to the Holy Spirit-inspired prophetic gift. Through chresmology, false prophets can have predictive prophecies and even have words of knowledge. *Oneiromancy* is the practice of interpreting dreams.[42] Though God can give the interpretation of dreams, oneiromancy is the divination counterpart. *Astrology* is where the stars and planets determine character, fate, and the future, in conjunction with the movements of the Zodiac.[43] *Necromancy* is the consultation with the dead, such as one with a familiar spirit who conducts séances.[44] These are just a few of the more popular methods of divination.

The false prophet in the previous chapter kept reassuring the audience that he was a legitimate prophet, but he let it slip that his specialty would be to know *times, dates, names, and conditions in people's bodies*. These are not the characteristics of a true prophet. Where in the Bible do you have a prophet of the Lord with these characteristics? *Observer of times* covers most of what divination seeks to do, unlock through demonic aid the mysteries behind the significance of certain times and dates, whether past or future. According to the Scriptures, this is an abomination before the Lord.

It is also interesting to note that the false prophet said that he would know "names." Discerning names is a common psychic technique. As we continue our study in upcoming chapters of the methods used by false prophets, we will move away from superficial gimmicks that many use to the more in-depth supernatural involvement.

THE CON GAME

In any con game, there is a system. A successful con man uses keen skills to discern whom to target. Con men are experts at picking their marks by reading certain characteristics such as facial and body language. Without uttering a word, the clothes we wear, our posture, and many other facets about our personality all communicate to the world who we are. Coming up in Chicago, many years ago, I use to take public transportation to and from school. On the buses you would see the *3-card-molly* con men working in teams of two or three. They would lay out three playing cards and allow you to get a good look at them. Then they told you to "pick a card." Let's say you chose the *3 of spades;* then they would flip over the cards, shuffle them around and tell you to touch the card you picked. Whatever card you touch, they flip it over. If it is the 3 of spades, you win twenty dollars. Easy enough, right? Wrong! His partner would pretend to be that curious onlooker on the bus that steps up, plays, and wins. Seeing someone win suspends others' disbelief. This is called *the setup.*

> *False prophets claim that they are building the kingdom of God, when in reality they are building their own kingdom, which is nothing more than a mechanism for their own well-being and financial prosperity.*

In this case, the 3-card-molly player may not be sure who is interested until they pull off the setup. Then they watch to see who is paying attention. Who did they captivate? But most importantly, whose greed will compel them to believe that they can beat the con man at his own game? It may only be one out of twenty, but that one they do get, they will take for all they can. This is the whole concept behind gambling casinos and lotteries—exploiting people's greed and taking their money. Just as people who are itching to make a fast buck fall prey to these type of schemes, so do greedy Christians looking for a spiritual thrill get taken in by false prophets. They are nothing more than spiritual 3-card-molly players looking to get into someone's pocket.

They prey on the "silly women (men too) laden with sins, and led away with divers lusts" (2 Tim.3:6, KJV, emphasis mine). In this text, these women (and others like them) were not only silly and gullible, but their conscience was weighed down by the guilt of their sins. Though they claimed to want God in their life, they wanted Him on their terms. This is why they could not hear from God and needed to hear a word from a false prophet. The following are some ways you can know a false prophet by their fruit.

EIGHT WAYS TO KNOW A FALSE PROPHET

1. *A false prophet will go out of their way to convince people they are a legitimate prophet.* This is part of the setup. They tout themselves as being the "true prophet," while they put down the other false prophets. They claim that signs and wonders follow them, and that they are eighty and ninety percent accurate. All this is fluff to get your confidence so that you will believe every word they speak. They will claim that Jesus has appeared to them. That they consult with or see angels. One prophet stated that an angel appeared to their mother and prophesied, "saying that your son is going to be a prophet." They have even entered into heavenly places, and so on. They say all this not only to impress you but so that you will believe all that they are telling you, so that you will submit to their so-called authority. False prophets cannot tolerate people that have the audacity to challenge their office and authority. A true prophet already knows that a wicked person is not going to receive their prophecy anyway. This is why prophets were unpopular, because "what thus sayeth the Lord" is usually different than "what the people want to hear." The prophet Micaiah told King Ahab, "You are going to die in this battle, and if you come back here tomorrow alive, then you will know that I am a false prophet"(My paraphrase; see 1 Kings 22). False prophets feel compelled to convince you that they are legitimate. This is a method that all liars and con artists use. It's like the sales technique used to combat a buyer's uncertainty about a product. The salesperson will say, "I have this model at home myself." People will lie to get you to buy.

2. *A false prophet will manipulate people into believing that they need the prophet.* They make you dependent upon their prognostications and say that without them, you cannot hear from God, because God will speak to them about you. False prophets always want to be your answer. They will twist the Scriptures and teach you

according to their rhema word. They always claim God is speaking to them, which gives them divine authority over others.

   3. ***Those providing prophecy on demand, is a tipoff they are not hearing from God.*** Prophecy is not an on demand gift, because it is administered as the Holy Spirit wills. Since it is God that speaks through the prophet that means the prophet is not in control of when they receive a prophetic message. A prophet must wait on the Lord. The prophet has no idea when, or about whom the Lord will speak to him about next. In his indictment to the false prophets God said, "Then the LORD said unto me, The prophets prophesy lies in my name: I sent them not, neither have I commanded them, neither spake unto them: they prophesy unto you a false vision and divination, and a thing of nought, and the deceit of their heart (Jeremiah 14:14, KJV). Here, the whole idea is, a legitimate prophet has to be called to be a prophet and sent by God with a prophecy that God Himself has spoken. The fact that authentic prophecy must originate from God, means that there is no one that knows beforehand when God will release a prophetic word to them.

This is important because, when a prophet is invited to a meeting like a prophetic conference, he or she is expected to prophesy during that conference, meaning, give a specific word of prophecy from the Lord to individuals at that conference. These prophets who tout how accurate they are, call people out for a specific prophetic "word from the Lord." Since a prophet doesn't know when God is going to speak to them from one day to the next, then certainly, they wouldn't know that months in advance either. However, the prophet is on the hook and expected to "perform" prophetically, regardless. Therefore, the prophet is forced to prophesy in the name of the Lord, when God has not spoken to them.

Just as no one knows when their cell phone will ring, even more so, no one can know the next time the Spirit will call on them to speak prophetically. If a prophet can conjure up prophecy at will, chances are they are operating in *chresmology* (see page 92), the divination counterpart to the biblical gift of prophecy. Here is what the Scripture emphatically state, "For no prophecy ever originated because some man willed it [to do so—it never came by human impulse], but men spoke from God who were borne along (moved and impelled) by the Holy Spirit" (2 Peter 1:21, AMP).

4. False prophets seek celebrity and make a show of how successful they have become. They flaunt their suits, their cars, their jewelry, their jets, and their mansions. They need celebrity status in order to be booked at the major church conferences and events to keep a following and stay in demand. Now, am I saying that there can be no wealthy believers or ministers? Of course not. Again, I am only talking about "false prophets." There are many blessed people in the kingdom of God. For the blessing of the Lord maketh rich and addeth no sorrow with it (Prov.10:22). Although in this text, rich does not only mean material wealth. However, by flaunting their success, false prophets make you covet what they have, and of course the way they will subscribe that you too will become rich is by *sowing a seed, and reaping a harvest.* When they ask you to sow a seed, they usually say that you are sowing a seed to God, who will in return release blessings such as *supernatural debt cancellation.* This is too good to be true. All you have to do is give to a prophet and your bills will be canceled? Think about it. Why would God cancel a debt like a car note, mortgage, credit card payment, etc., that you lawfully owe? The Bible declares, "The wicked borroweth, and payeth not again…" (Psalm 37:21, KJV).

In 2 Kings 4:1-7, for the widow that was in debt to creditors who were going to enslave her sons, Elisha didn't promise that the Lord was going to supernaturally cancel her debt that she legally owed. But what he did do was miraculously increase what she did have (a pot of oil), so she could sell it to *pay off* her debts and have extra. Now in a case where the debt is an unrighteous debt, through being swindled or a an extortioner comes to force somebody to pay money they really don't owe, I believe that God can be merciful and bring deliverance in cases like these. However, God *is not* canceling debts because you *sow a seed* to a false prophet. This is a con game to get your money. We all want our bills to go away, right? And they will, as soon as you pay them off!

Besides, what about the businesses that have rendered a service to you? Don't they need their money? What if someone owed you money or owed the prophet money? Would they want those debts canceled too? In the year of Jubilee, all debts are forgiven simultaneously. The entire economy is reset. This way no one is hurt, because everyone owes somebody something, so it balances out. (A nation that wants real economic reform should practice Jubilee. Forgive everyone's debts across the board every fifty years, and you'll have a perpetually robust economy.) But to prophesy that you will receive supernatural debt cancellation because you sow a seed is just plain foolishness. No, after you sow that seed, you are still going to have to pay your car note, rent, mortgage, and credit card bills. Oh yes, a lot of these false prophets will let you go further into debt by allowing you to sow that abundant seed on your credit card! Maybe they expect that after they collect the money from the credit card transaction, God will supernaturally hit the delete key on the credit card company's computer to make the debt go away for you. If anything, your financial woes will worsen because you believed the words of a deceiver.

Finally, a passage of Scripture you will never hear false prophets (false profits) quote is, "He who oppresses the poor to make more for himself or who gives to the rich, *will* only *come to poverty*" (Prov. 22:16, NASB). Many Christians do not know that *"those who give to the rich will become poor."* Many of these false prophets are wealthy, but they oppress the poor by taking money from them. Others who are better off and can afford to give do so because they are covetous for more and believe that when they sow a seed to the prophet who drove up in a Bentley, they are sowing into good ground. No, it's not good ground, because they are false. The Bible declares, if you give to the rich, you shall come to poverty.

5. *False prophets are always self-centered. It's always about them.* Jesus' name is secondary, while their name is primary. It's all about exploiting people to promote *their brand* and draw a following after themselves. Their name is always foremost, not Jesus' name. They always claim that they are building the kingdom of God, when in reality they are building their own kingdom, which is nothing more than a mechanism for their own well-being and financial prosperity. They proclaim, "Come to my service," "come to my prophetic conference," "come to my anniversary," "come to my birthday," "come hear a word that I'm about to give you." With the false prophet it's always me, myself, and I, with Jesus' name thrown in for authenticity purposes, but make no mistake about it, it's all about self promotion. Here is what the apostle Paul said: "Even some men from your own group will rise up and distort the truth in order to draw a following. Watch out!" (Acts 20:29-31, NLT)

6. *Prophecies from false prophets are notoriously vague.* Their prophecies can mean anything or nothing while sounding profound and deep. Their lying words bring forth nothing. In the book of Jude, here is what it says about the substance of false prophets:

> These are spots in your feasts of charity, when they feast with you, feeding themselves without fear; clouds they are without water, carried about of winds; trees whose fruit withereth, without fruit, twice dead, plucked up by the roots; Raging waves of the sea, foaming out their own shame; wandering stars, to whom is reserved the blackness of darkness for ever.
>
> Jude 12-13, KJV

Jude uses specific metaphors loaded with meaning as he describes false prophets. *Clouds without rain* is a metaphor that would be especially meaningful to a nation such as Israel. Droughts are a significant threat to the survival of any agricultural society. In the midst of a famine, there is nothing more disappointing than clouds without rain. On one hand they are promising, but the end result is they give nothing, just being blown aimlessly by the wind.

False prophets proclaim meaningless words like, "God is about to do something in your life." "The Lord is shifting some things around." "Things are getting ready to happen." "The Lord says, people are against you and don't like you, but don't worry about them, the Lord sees them." "I see increase coming your way, from the north, south, east, and west." "People are jealous of you, but don't let them discourage you." "There are hindrances in the atmosphere, but God is moving them out of the way." "I see angels in the room right now, and they are here to bring deliverance." These are just some of the nebulous folly that you hear coming from the lips of these false prophets.

When speaking of false prophets, Jesus said, "you will know them by their fruits." That means false prophets themselves are discernible. They like to shroud themselves in mystery, but their fruits will give them away. They make vague prognostications because they are not hearing from God, and cannot be specific or give any great detail because God has not spoken to them. Just imagine Jesus telling the woman at Jacob's Well, "I see some things in the atmosphere getting ready to happen. Get me some water, and you will receive a prophet's reward. Be a blessing to the prophet and sow a seed and you will receive increase in your life one-hundred-fold! I see a new chariot and some new robes in your future. And by the way, there is a fulfilling relationship about to happen in your life."

Of course we know this is not what Jesus said to this woman. The Lord, nor any true prophet, does not play games with people's lives. Jesus was concerned about this woman's soul. He was concerned about the sinful life that she was living. He dealt directly with her sin and was very specific. "You have had five husbands, and the man you are with now is not your husband." Think about it. Why would God send a prophet to someone to prophesy about receiving material wealth when they have a sin-sick soul as we find this woman to have? No, Jesus dealt with her sin so she could be free from the penalty of sin and death, and experience the true wealth found in salvation and eternal life.

However, the main reason false prophets are vague is because it protects them from going out on a limb where they can be clearly identified as making a false prophecy. Vagueness is intentional to protect their status and gives them a back-door exit if things do not come to pass as they prophesied. A false prophet never wants to give a prophecy where they can be held accountable and cornered for giving a lying prophecy. If they are caught giving a false prophecy, they will claim that they are not perfect. However, whenever a prophet prefaces their prophecy with "thus saith the Lord" or words to that effect, there is no room for error, because they are saying that the Lord spoke this directly to them. You only get wiggle room when a prophet says, "I believe this or that is going to happen." But they don't want to say it like that, because they want to give you the impression that what they say has come from God. However, you do not get any margin of error when you make a prophecy "in the Lord's name" when He did not tell you to speak. Not only are you making yourself out to be a liar, but you are making God a liar too, because you're saying He said it. And last but not least, you have taken the Lord's name in vain, by using his name to proclaim something that he did not say. This is what the Word of the Lord declares:

> But the prophet who presumes to speak a word in My name which I have not commanded him to speak, or who speaks in the name of other gods, **that same prophet shall die.** And if you say in your [minds and] hearts, How shall we know which words the Lord has not spoken? When a prophet speaks in the name of the Lord, if the word does not come to pass or prove true, that is a word which the Lord has not spoken. The prophet has spoken it presumptuously; you shall not be afraid of him.

> Deuteronomy 18:20-22, AMP

Make all the excuses you want. God does not take it lightly when people prophesy falsely in His name, period! But on occasion you get one of these *so-called* prophets that does make a specific prophecy that proves false. Such was the case of a nationally known prophet, touted as being one of the most accurate, made a definite prophecy, claiming that the Lord said, "Trump is just a decoy and that he will not be president." Of course, we all know that Donald Trump became president. This false prophet did something that they normally do not do, is make a specific prophesy that can be proven to be false.

7. False prophets rely on gimmicks to attract and stir up the people, to fool the people into believing that the false prophet has powers. This is different from a preacher that uses illustrations during a service to give additional emphasis to his sermon or lesson. These gimmicks are trickery specifically designed to show that the prophet is supernatural. The documentary *Marjoe*, produced by Marjoe Gortner in 1972, is a film about how he deceived people his whole life by conducting sham revivals all over the country for decades. He started as a boy, exploited by his parents to preach and prophesy since early childhood, but he never believed in God himself, nor was he a Christian, even though he drew thousands at revivals all over the country.

On one occasion he spoke of drawing a cross on his forehead with some special ink. When this ink interacted with the sweat on his forehead, a blood-red cross appeared, and the people were amazed. He said that preachers had to have a gimmick, whether it was saying that they could heal people, or have a word of knowledge, or prophesy. They had to bring a gimmick in order to draw the crowds or they would never be booked at the big conferences. Having a great gimmick made it easy to take offerings and make money.[45] This is so sad. So many people that think they are on the road to heaven have entered onto the broad road that leads to destruction. Jesus warned of this when he said, "Enter through the narrow gate. For wide is the gate and broad is the road that leads to destruction, and many enter through it. But small is the gate and narrow the road that leads to life and only a few find it" (Matt.7:13-14).

8. *False prophets often change their name to a biblical character's name.* In some schools of prophets (particularly the ones that teach divination), they are taught that they must change their name to a "prophetic name." Prophetic name is usually a name of a biblical character or location. They do this because angels and demons, as they insist, only respond to certain names. This erroneous teaching is based on what the demon said to Sceva and his sons, "Jesus I know, and Paul I know, but who are you" (Acts 19:13-20). This concept is also based on God changing individuals; names in Scripture, like Abram to Abraham, or Jacob to Israel, or Saul to Paul. Of course this is ridiculous and another example of the deceitful use of Scripture, because in cases like Abraham, Isaac, and Jacob, none of these were self-initiated name changes, besides the fact that the vast majority of prophets' names were not changed.

Secondly, and most importantly, false prophets also assert that without the prophetic name, spirit entities will not be subject to them, nor can they gain access to them, which is necessary for receiving information from spirits. Therefore, when you encounter these prophets that have adopted names found in the Bible, that is a tipoff that a prophet *may have* been trained in this mystical philosophy from one of these schools of prophets. Without belaboring this point, there is only one name that things in heaven (angels), things on earth (humans), or things under the earth (demons) respond or bow to; that's the name of Jesus!

Your prophets have seen for you false and deceptive visions;
they have not exposed your iniquity to restore your fortunes,
but have seen for you oracles that are false and misleading.
Lamentations 2:14, ESV

CHAPTER SIX

DIGGING A LITTLE DEEPER
HOW DO THEY DO IT?

not long ago, while conducting research for this book, I ran across a most interesting psychic website, where they give tips on how not to be fooled by *fake psychics*. Here is what they said: "If the Psychic asks you a lot of questions, this is called a cold reading, and it is never accurate. A *true* psychic should never have to ask you more than your *name and birthday* to give you a real psychic reading."[46] I thought this was very interesting. In order to do a good psychic reading on someone, they need information such as your name and date of birth.

As we covered in the previous chapter, *numerology* is the part of divination where readings are done on a person using their *name* and *birth date*. Each letter of a person's name is given a numerical equivalent. The vowels are added up and then the consonants. Those totals and the birth date, when added together, are called the "destiny number," and all those numbers are then charted in order to complete a personality reading.

According to the *Foretune-Teller's Bible, The Definitive Guide to the Arts of Divination*, this system also works on any name, even for a business or sports team. I also found it interesting that within the scope of divination is focusing on *reaching your destiny*. Over the last couple decades, we've been hearing a lot about Christians reaching their destiny atconferences, in books and in sermonic material. Whereas there may be no intended connection to divination, fads quickly attach to our way of thinking and end up in coming over in our preaching and teaching. Reaching your destiny sounds great. It's a great sound bite, and it gets people excited, but we often fail to ask, "Where did this buzz phrase orignate, from the Bible?" A Christian's destiny is where they have their citizenship, which is heaven (Phil. 3:20). We are seated in heavenly places with Him (Eph. 2:6). The Lord Himself is coming back for us to take us to the place that He has prepared for us (John 14:1-4). That's our true destiny. Everything else on this earth is temporal and shall pass away. During the time that we live on earth, it's all about fulfilling our calling, purpose, and our service to the Lord. This is why the Scriptures admonish us to "Set your minds (affections) on things above, not on earthly things" (Colossians 3:2). Again, I am not suggesting that a minister that emphasizes reaching your destiny, is wittingly espousing tenets of divination.

I began walking down this road for a reason. Not long ago I found a website of this so-called "Master Prophet," whom I will keep anonymous. Why? Because vultures look alike, knowing their name isn't necessary, knowing their tactics are what is important. On his website, he speaks of receiving a "free prophecy from the master prophet." So I couldn't resist. I signed up using a deceased relative's name. In order to receive my *personal prophecy* from the master prophet, besides an email address, guess what information he asked for? A *name and birthday.* Sound familiar? This is exactly what the psychic said is needed in order to complete a *psychic reading.* Where in the Bible does a prophet ask for someone's name or birth date? Where did he get that from?

What I am about to share is the word-for-word communication from this lying false prophet that was sent back to me via email. However, before I do, let's look again at the main premise of this book taken from the Mount Olivet discourse, where Jesus warned,

> As Jesus was sitting on the Mount of Olives, the disciples came to him privately. "Tell us," they said, "when will this happen, and what will be the sign of your coming and of the end of the age?" Jesus answered: "Watch out that no one deceives you…and many false prophets will appear and deceive many people. For false messiahs

and false prophets will appear and perform great signs and wonders to deceive, if possible, even the elect." Matt. 24:3-4,11,24

When thinking of the end times, we cannot overlook the emergence of false prophets as among the other telling signs of the end times. This by itself is alarming, because false prophets have always caused problems throughout the millenia, but during the last days the floodgates will be flung open and false prophets will be everywhere, particularly in certain Christian churches. However, in this age of technological expansion where the internet has transformed our day-to-day functioning, false prophets have really capitalized on various social media outlets to give them national and even global reach. Now there are internet trolls who call themselves prophets, who have one purpose in mind, which is to exploit weak-minded and vulnerable individuals for their money, doing it all in the name of Jesus.

THE EMAIL PROPHET

In the previous chapter we discussed eight ways to tell a false prophet. We will see some of these play out in the following discourse. After sending the required name and birthday to the false prophet's website, I received an email rather quickly. Here is what the first email said:

Jonathan, YOU CAN CHANGE YOUR CIRCUM-STANCES TODAY!

"Surely the Lord God will do nothing, but he revealeth his secret unto his servants the prophets." (Amos 3:7)

Dear Jonathan

Praise the Lord! As your personal prophet, I want to thank you so much for requesting your personal prophecy. I know this word will be a blessing to you.

Jonathan, whose report will you believe? The scriptures tell us that the Lord God will do nothing *"but he revealeth his secret unto his servants the prophets."* Know this! The prophet is the voice of God in the earth called to bring man back into right relationship with Him. God uses the prophet to bring direction, clarity, and definition to His people.

Jonathan, COULD I TELL YOU THAT YOUR CHANGE IS NEAR?

You'll be surprised to learn that true prophets preach for change; and those who are attracted to the prophetic have reached a point in life where change is compulsory. Jonathan, I see change on the horizon for you! **I want to send your life-changing prophetic word via email within 48 hours.**

Let's unpack this email. First of all, let's keep in mind that the person that they are communicating with is deceased, which means there is nothing authentically prophetic to this at all, but is simply a scam. However, notice that this false prophet markets himself as "your personal prophet," which is a similar marketing technique used by other psychics, palm readers, and others who operate in the divination deception. Having one's own personal prophet plays on a person's ego to make them feel good about themselves, like they are special. Everyone wants something they can call their own, especially when that someone can give them "a word" whenever it is needed. However, the real purpose is to cause the person to become dependent on the prophet to the point where the person receiving prophecies will call the prophet before making any decisions.

To fortify their value, the prophet then uses *"Surely the Lord God will do nothing, but he revealeth his secret unto his servants the prophets"* (Amos

3:7). In other words, I am the prophet. God speaks to me about you. Therefore, you need me as your personal prophet in order to get a word from the Lord concerning directions for your life. Remember, Jesus speaking of false prophets said, "you will know them by their fruits" (Matt. 7:15-20). The email goes on to say,

> Jonathan, whose report will you believe? The scriptures tell us that the Lord God will do nothing *but he revealeth his secret unto his servants the prophets."* Know this! The prophet is the voice of God in the earth called to bring man back into right relationship with Him. God uses the prophet to bring direction, clarity, and definition to His people.

In the previous chapter, I list eight ways that you can know a false prophet. Already, in the first few sentences of this email we see: *#2 A false prophet will manipulate people into believing that they need the prophet.* Listen to the emphasis he places after the statement "God will do nothing *but he revealeth his secret unto his servants the prophets."* He punctuates that statement with, "know This!" This is to put emphasis on the fact that you need *him* to hear a word from the Lord on your behalf. These techniques are designed to soften up the recipient so that the prophet can bring *direction, clarity, and definition* to someone's life. Meaning that the prophet has a hand in defining where you go in life, how to think about where you are going in life, while defining who you are and who you will become through his prophetic influence and insight. This is nothing more than a trickster's attempt to insert mind control over some vulnerable individual.

The next paragraph in the email follows:

Jonathan, COULD I TELL YOU THAT YOUR CHANGE IS NEAR?

You'll be surprised to learn that true prophets preach for change; and those who are attracted to the prophetic have reached a point in life where change is compulsory. Jonathan, I see change on the horizon for you! **I want to send your life-changing prophetic word via email within 48 hours.**

Again, we see that the prophet reassures that he is a "true prophet." This coincides with #1 *"A false prophet will always convince people to believe that he or she is a legitimate prophet."* However, notice what he says next, "those who are attracted to the prophetic have reached a point in life where change is compulsory." In other words, certain people are predisposed to seek out prophets when they are confused and cannot find answers to the questions about their life. Usually people that fit this psychological profile have several issues such as significant failures or loss in life, are prone to depression, have low self-esteem, and have unrealistic expectations of how change in life occurs. Though they don't want to cross the line and consult a psychic, they feel safe with a prophet of the Lord. Since they are weighted down with so many burdens, they think that by consulting a prophet they can take a shortcut through the vicissitudes of life. Some people are looking for someone to lead them, and that's exactly what any false prophet or cult leader is looking for, someone who will give the false prophet control over their life. These needy souls are looking for someone else to define them, but instead of being defined they get used, because the false prophet is only concerned about their own self interests and welfare. Next the false prophet says,

> Jonathan, don't delay! You are walking into self-mastery in this season, but you must be aware of everything that God is trying to reveal to you in this season. Remember, destiny is not left up to chance, but it is a matter of choice.

Just about any product that is being sold on television always tells you to hurry and respond now. This is a marketing technique used to capitalize on a person's excitement to spark impulse-buying. In this case, it is to entice engagement. God has something that He wants to reveal to Jonathan, but instead of revealing it to Jonathan, God is going to reveal it to the prophet, and the prophet will reveal it to Jonathan through a personal prophecy, from his "personal prophet," but he has to respond in forty-eight hours! Then the false prophet makes this statement, *"Remember, destiny is not left up to chance, but it is a matter of choice."* That sounds great, right? Well, let's see where the philosophy behind this statement comes from.

The statement below is taken directly from a Chinese fortune-teller's website:

> According to the Chinese belief our fate is not inevitable, our actions can alter our destiny. Where we are coming from and where we are going is determined by the interactions of Heaven Chi, Earth Chi and Man Chi. Chinese astrology helps us to understand those forces and their patterns, so we'll be able to choose— use our free will—which path we will walk in our journey of life.[47]

Notice the key words are *choice* and *destiny*. Though I am not saying this false prophet takes his concepts from this website, but the philosophy of reaching your destiny by one's choice has deep roots in divination. In contrast, the Scriptures declare, "The steps of a good man are ordered by the Lord" (Ps.37:23, NKJV), "the Lord is the author and finisher of our faith" (Heb. 11:2, NKJV), "And we know that all things work together for good to those who love God, to those who are the called according to *His* purpose. For whom He foreknew, He also 'predestined' *to be* conformed to the image of His Son…" (Rom. 8:28-30, NKJV)."…just as He chose us in Him before the foundation of the world, that we should be holy and without blame before Him in love, having "predestined" us to adoption as sons by Jesus Christ to Himself, according to the good pleasure of His will…"(Eph. 1:4-5, NKJV). "And do not be conformed to this world, but be transformed by the renewing of your mind, that you may prove what *is* that good and acceptable and perfect will of God" (Rom. 12:2, NKJV). It's not so much about you finding *your* destiny; it's about you finding out what is God's will for your life. The clay doesn't say to the potter, make me like this or shape me like that (Rom. 9:20-23). Remember, God is the potter, we are the clay. You seeking your own destiny will lead you to destruction, and it leaves you open to be deceived by a false prophet's guidance. The Bible declares, "Trust in the LORD with all your heart, And lean not on your own understanding; In all your ways acknowledge Him, And He shall direct your paths. There is a way *that seems* right to a man, But its end *is* the way of death" (Proverbs 3:5-6, 16:25, NKJV). Blessed is the man that walketh not in the counsel of the ungodly... (Psalm 1:1, KJV).

The reason I offered information from the *Chinese fortune-teller's* website is because, as we have already extensively covered, fortune-telling is a practice of divination. Divination is what Scriptures declare is what false prophets practice. These divination concepts are very similar ones that the false prophet is using. Seeking one's destiny is an integral part of divination, because divination/fortune-telling seeks information about the wealth and prosperity in one's future or destiny. However, as we can see from the passages above, choosing your own destiny *is not* what the Bible teaches. What the Bible teaches is that we are *pre*-destined according to the good pleasure of God's will, not ours. The Bible instructs us that we should not be conformed to this world, but be transformed by the renewing of our mind (Rom. 12:2).

What we know about psychics, astrologers, fortune-tellers, and the like is that they are mystical concepts based on tenets of divination that are forbidden by God. Not only that, the false prophet asks for a person's name and birth date, which is the same information the psychic website requests in order to conduct a psychic reading on an individual. This is important, because the false prophet's website requires a name and birth date before they will send the personal prophecy back to you.

Why is all of this important, and what does this have to do with our study? Let's examine another passage that can help us unpack this pressing question.

> The word of the LORD came to me: "Son of man, prophesy against the prophets of Israel who are now prophesying. Say to those who prophesy out of their own imagination: 'Hear the word of the LORD!' This is what the Sovereign LORD says: Woe to the foolish prophets who follow their own spirit and have seen nothing!… Their visions are false and their **divinations** a lie. Even though the LORD has not sent them, they say, 'The LORD declares,' and expect him to fulfill their words. Have you not seen false visions and uttered lying **divinations** when you say, 'The LORD declares,' though I have not spoken?"
>
> Ezekiel 13:1-7

Without the slightest doubt, this passage clearly says that false prophets are liars that use *divination*. This is not my assertion simply because I have some point to make. God is saying this! This is why it must be exposed for what it is. Many of the people running around today calling themselves prophets are fulfilling the end-time prophecy, "that many false prophets will arise and deceive many." Many of these so-called prophets are being mentored by, as the subject of our case study calls himself, a master prophet. This deceiver also has a "School of the Prophets" where he teaches the "science of prophecy" and has a course on miracles. The people who attend schools sponsored and taught by a false prophet(s) will also learn divination techniques that are being passed off as Kingdom of God principles, and Holy Spirit movement. They learn how to call out people's name, phone numbers, and addresses (more on this later), which impresses people that are ignorant of divination practices and techniques.

Finally, back to our "personal prophecy email." In the postscript of the email this is what the master prophet says,

> "P.S.S. I want to see you wealthy! God wants you to become successful and wealthy!"

Really? God wants us to be wealthy? Without a doubt, there are Scriptures that support abundance, increase, blessing, and good success, but there are also Scriptures that warn about the deceitfulness of riches. However, most importantly, there are no scriptures that encourage people to *pursue* riches of this world.

In the following passages, you will get an understanding about what the Bible teaches about those who covet wealth. *You cannot serve God and money* (Luke 16:13), *the deceitfulness of riches chokes out the Word* (Matt. 13:22), *Those who want to be rich pierce themselves with many sorrows* (1 Tim. 6:9-11), *the difficulty of a rich man entering the Kingdom* (Mark 10:25), *Warning against those that trust in riches* (Ps. 49:6-20), *labor not to be rich* (Prov. 23:4), *a poor righteous man is better off than the rich wicked* (Prov. 28:6), *Hasty to be rich* (Prov. 28:6), *The harsh warning James has to the rich* (James 1:10-11, 2:6, 5:1-6), *The Church of Laodicea rebuked because their wealth had affected their relationship with Christ* (Rev. 3:17-19).

Jesus never taught anyone to seek worldly wealth. However, he does teach seek first the kingdom of God, and His righteousness and all the things will be added to you. It is true that the blessing of the Lord maketh rich and adds no sorrow, but rich here means more than money. Particularly in America, in a capitalistic society where people's wealth and possessions define the individual, we place a lot of emphasis on obtaining wealth and often interpret the Bible within that framework. Everyone is simply not going to be a millionaire, nor does the Bible teach such. As a matter of fact, Jesus quoting from Deut. 15:11, stated, "The poor you shall always have with you" (Matt. 26:11).

The Follow up Email

In the follow up email, the master prophet goes directly for the wallet. Here's what he writes:

> I must be completely honest with you; I was overjoyed to make contact with you because I could sense your hesitancy, your inner doubt and your slightness of fear concerning your belief in the prophet and I couldn't wait to write you back because I knew you had questions and doubts. The moment I sensed this about you was the moment I heard the Lord say, "Jonathan must learn how to walk away from people and situations that threaten Jonathan's peace of mind, self-respect and self-worth!"

This liar is relentless! Ironically, he actually starts his statement with, "I must be completely honest with you...," before he starts lying. Remember, this is to my deceased relative. However, the prophet says, "I could sense your hesitancy, your inner doubt and your slightness of fear concerning your belief in the prophet." Notice the prophet reinforces a belief in "the prophet," not in God.

Remember, the true prophet is a mouthpiece for God. Again, this is grooming so the prophet can *make a profit,* when he goes for the wallet. Then he says, "I heard the Lord say, 'Jonathan must learn how to walk away from people and situations that threaten Jonathan's peace of mind, self-respect and self-worth!'" Again, this is a clear example of a false prophet lying in the name of the Lord. He claims, "I heard the Lord saying...." The Lord hasn't said anything to my dead relative. This is a blatant lie. However, what the false prophet is attempting to do is to get someone to separate themselves from anyone who would discourage them from being advised by the false prophet. The false prophet then lies on the Lord and says he heard the Lord saying, "Jonathan must learn how to walk away..." That's interesting. Even if the prophet didn't know my relative was deceased, wouldn't the Lord know? This is exactly what Jeremiah and Ezekiel say false prophets do: they lie in the Lord's name even though He has not spoken to them. The false prophet goes on to say:

> These things have caused you to believe non-sense like, "my life isn't fair", "I'm just unlucky"… However Jonathan, it could all change when you believe the prophet…You could suddenly inherit thousands of dollars in CASH as a result of hearing one prophetic word from the Lord about a contact.

Here, the false prophet casts the lure of becoming instantly wealthy. Notice he puts "cash" in all caps. Of course this won't happen unless the prophet hears from the Lord on your behalf. After grooming Jonathan with these two emails, the false prophet is ready to strike for the wallet. Look how this snake does it. He actually uses a Scriptural reference to solicit the money:

> God said it…

> Believe in the Lord your God, so shall ye be established; believe his prophets, so shall ye prosper. II Chronicles **20:20.** Today, I want you to take another step towards your future. You've made monumental progress through contacting me alone. Now it's time to take one giant, revolutionary step into your future.

> Alert me now and click the little blue link below to notify me personally that you are ready to **BELIEVE THE PROPHET** and all that I ask is that you make a simple investment in your future with a special **"I BELIEVE THE PROPHET" faith seed of $20.20 for II Chronicles 20:20.**

Now we finally get to what this lying prophet was really after all the time. This deceiver has no shame. He will lie on God and lie to people to their face. He twists the Scriptures to manipulate and con people out of their money without any concern for wrecking someone's finances or faith. But he will sleep just fine, because anyone who carries on a fraud like this obviously has a reprobate mind and is void of conviction. Here is what the Scriptures declare about false prophets:

> Her leaders issue rulings for a bribe, her priests teach for payment, and her prophets practice divination for money. Yet they lean on the LORD, saying, "Isn't the LORD among us? No disaster will overtake us."
>
> Micah 3:11, HCSB

This passage hits the nail on the head when it comes to calling out people like the master prophet. The statement that "her prophets practice divination for money" is direct and explicit, revealing the true motivation behind wanting money and authority through the exploitation of the people. This is so sad, because on Judgment Day, these same liars will stand before the Lord and say, "...Lord, Lord, did we not prophesy in your name...then I will tell them plainly, 'I never knew you. Away from me, you evildoers!'" (Matt.7:22-23) Imagine, if 100 people respond to this $20.20, that's $2,020. If a thousand respond, that's $20,200, and so on. You get the point! False prophets are relentless and unrepentant. Since they are not hearing from the Lord, they are either prophesying out of their own deluded minds, or they are under the influence of a far darker power.

Another incident occurred in 2014 when a nationally known prophet was caught giving prophecies that were almost word for word predictions from an internet psychic for the year 2015. One of the predictions that the psychic made was that President George H.W. Bush would get sick and die in 2015. The prophet repeated all of the psychic's predictions, including the Bush's demise prophecy. As of July 2018, Bush senior is still with us. In some circles, this controversy caused a big stir about the prophet quoting a psychic. Though the retort and denial from the prophet were vehement, ironically the denial works against the prophet. If he did quote the psychic, that would have at least given him a reason why he was wrong. The problem is if the prophecy about Bush didn't come from the psychic, and it obviously did not come from God, then where did it originate? When you operate in divination, you are hearing from lying spirits when you think you're hearing from God.

CHAPTER SEVEN

COUNTERFEIT CHARISMA

THE DARK POWER

*A*s we continue our study of the role that divination plays in the workings of the false prophet, we will find that it is not always easy to distinguish between the counterfeit and the genuine. On one hand, it's simpler to tell the difference between a false prophecy and a legitimate word of prophecy by the fulfillment itself. In general, if the prophecy comes true, then it was a legitimate prophecy. If it doesn't come to pass, then it wasn't a prophecy from the Lord. However, what if a false prophet declares a prophecy or produces a sign that *does* come true? What shall we do in that case? Let's turn to the Scriptures to answer this question:

> Suppose there are prophets among you or those who dream dreams about the future, and they promise you signs or miracles, and the predicted signs or miracles occur. If they then say, "Come, let us worship other gods"—gods you have not known before—do not listen to them. The LORD your God is testing you to see if you truly love him with all your heart and soul.
>
> Deuteronomy 13:1-3, NLT

In this passage the Lord instructs His people concerning false prophets that can work signs and wonders that actually *do* come to pass. This is important, because in the churches where false prophets operate,

> *Practices such as divination, do not always come over as demonic. This is why Simon the Sorcerer had so much influence because the people claimed that he was "the great power of God."*

the people are amazed by how accurate these false prophets can be. However, accuracy alone is not the only factor to consider. This is why you cannot be impressed by someone who calls out your name, address, phone number, or knows some bits of information about you. But you must also discern what is their message. Does it line up with the whole counsel of the Scriptures? Is it mixed with false doctrine or tenets of occultism, or does it utilize principles and practices of things like divination which the Bible forbids. Does it lead you to accept a false gospel by those who use the Scriptures deceitfully?

Though the New Testament clearly embraces the prophetic gift, tight usage in the church was imposed to help prevent the spread of erroneous doctrine. For example, in 1 Cor. 14:29-30, the Bible instructs, "Let the prophets speak two or three, and let the other judge. If *anything* be revealed to another that sitteth by, let the first hold his peace." In the Church, prophetic utterances were to be tested. The testing of prophetic utterances is also taught in 1 John 4:1,"Beloved, do not believe every spirit, but test the spirits, whether they are of God; because many false prophets have gone out into the world" (NKJV). This is important, because though some false prophets rely on trickery such as searching out information about people through social media, or getting information collected from conference registration forms, others are actually trafficking in the demonic, by teaching and promoting doctrines of demons. Here is what the Word of God warns, "Now the Spirit expressly says that in latter times some will depart from the faith, giving heed to deceiving spirits and doctrines of demons" (1 Tim.4:1, NKJV).

Doctrines of demons are very subtle, because they can be ever so close to the truth and pass right through a church as wholesome teaching. This is why Paul instructed the Corinthians that if a prophet (who can also serve as a teacher) has a word or revelation, it must be judged by others that also have that gift, to prevent the spread of false doctrine. False doctrine once received will ultimately pull you away from the faith. This is what the Lord also warned against in Deut.13:1-3, where the Scriptures identify the prophet whose prophecy or sign comes true, but leads you away from the Lord. This is a false prophet.

Peter called the doctrines that false teachers (prophets) bring with them *damnable heresies* or heresies that lead to destruction (2 Peter 2:1), because they too, draw you away from the Lord through false teaching. Though there are safeguards that must be in place when it comes to prophetic utterances, it is important not to overreact and throw the baby out with the bathwater. This is why the Bible also teaches, "Do not despise prophecies. Test all things; hold fast what is good" (1 Thess.5:20-21, NKJV).

According to the *Encyclopedia of Religious Phenomena*, in a few areas of divination, anyone with basic knowledge can practice. Other forms of divination require a specialist that has been trained, because astrology, tarot cards, and numerology have advanced levels. Additionally, divination is frequently practiced by some that have innate psychic and paranormal abilities.[48] There are many people that are born with this sixth sense, and throughout their lives have known or sensed things about people or events in the form of premonitions, dreams, and visions. Whereas many only dabble in divination at a superficial level, there are others that are given over to it and go far deeper than the typical person who reads their daily horoscope. However, whether these divination practitioners are fully involved as a career or as a novice, the Scriptures explicitly prohibit believers from taking part in divination at any level. Here is what the Bible says about these practices:

> *As a true prophet is the mouthpiece for God's prophetic revelation, so are mediums the mouthpiece for the spirits that speak through them.*
>
>

When you enter the land the LORD your God is giving you, do not learn to imitate the detestable ways of the nations there. Let no one be found among you who sacrifices their son or daughter in the fire, who practices divination or sorcery, interprets omens, engages in witchcraft, or casts spells, or who is a medium or spiritist or who consults the dead. Anyone who does these things is detestable to the LORD; because of these same detestable practices the LORD your God will drive out those nations before you. You must be blameless before the LORD your God.

Deuteronomy18:9-13

In the New Testament this is what the apostle Paul warns:

No, not at all. I am saying that these sacrifices are offered to demons, not to God. And I don't want you to participate with demons. You cannot drink from the cup of the Lord and from the cup of demons, too. You cannot eat at the Lord's Table and at the table of demons, too.

1 Corinthians 10:20-21, NLT

God's emphatic warning not to get involved in any type of divination practice is an indication that this is not some harmless activity. The Lord knows that the powers behind these mystical arts are demonic even though they might be intriguing and seem harmless. Practices such as divination do not always come across as demonic, but rather *as the power of God*. Again, the reason Simon the Sorcerer had so much influence was because the people claimed that he was "the great power of God." Satan always counterfeits the things pertaining to God so that he can deceive and snare those who have made themselves open to his influence through these occult practices.

In 1 Corinthians, Paul makes an astounding revelation concerning one of Satan's principal *modus operandi* to deceive and ultimately destroy people who do not understand that not all evil presents as such:

> And no wonder! For Satan himself transforms himself into an angel of light. Therefore *it is* no great thing if his ministers also transform themselves into ministers of righteousness, whose end will be according to their works.
> 2 Corinthians 11:14-15, NKJV

Angels of light, as Paul puts it here, is another metaphor for wolves in sheep's clothing. This means that some of these false prophets will perform signs and wonders, but not only in a three-ring circus or on the Vegas strip, but in the pews and pulpits of the local church. They will be the ones Paul speaks of as being Satan's ministers that are transformed into ministers of righteousness, with the specific assignment of operating in the Church and deceiving Christians.

THE SPIRIT OF DIVINATION

In the book of Acts, we have the case of the Philippian slave girl who was possessed with a spirit of divination that had "a word" for Paul and Silas:

> As we were on our way to the place of prayer, we were met by a slave girl who was possessed by a spirit of divination [claiming to foretell future events and to discover hidden knowledge], and she brought her owners much gain by her fortunetelling. She kept following Paul and [the rest of] us, shouting loudly, These men are the servants of the Most High God! They announce to you

> *Satan transforms himself into an angel of light to deceive people into believing that they are in the presence of God. False prophets believe that their gifts and powers are legitimate, when in reality they are counterfeit.*

the way of salvation! And she did this for many days. Then Paul, being sorely annoyed *and* worn out, turned and said to the spirit within her, I charge you in the name of Jesus Christ to come out of her! And it came out that very moment. But when her owners discovered that their hope of profit was gone, they caught hold of Paul and Silas and dragged them before the authorities in the forum (marketplace), [where trials are held].

Acts 16:16-19, AMP

Here, Dr. Luke introduces us to a young woman who had a "spirit of divination." She was not dealing at some superficial level, but this young lady was in deep. It is interesting how the Amplified Version expands the meaning of divination to include "foretell future events and to discover hidden knowledge." Being possessed with a demon gave her these powers. From this we can learn that spirits of divination supernaturally enable a person to know some things about the future, and to disclose knowledge that would otherwise be hidden. Hidden knowledge, such as a person's information, that others would not normally know.

In this case, this woman without any foreknowledge of Paul and Silas called out Paul and Silas' mission saying, "These men are the servants of the Most High God! They announce to you the way of salvation!" This woman under demonic influence knew who Paul and Silas were serving and why they came to Philippi. What she was doing back then is what false prophets are doing today. She called out Paul and Silas' mission, while today's false prophets call out your address and phone number. Like the false prophet that called out the man's address "5252," calling that a sign from the Lord. If we were to bring this same girl into the 21st century, clean her up, send her to a "school of prophets," put a Bible in her hand, and give her a pulpit to preach from, she would pack churches all over the country. Her power would be amazing, her words would be accurate, her sermons preached from a text in the Bible, and done in Jesus' name, with this one crucial distinction—she would be operating in demonic divination, not the Holy Spirit.

It is interesting that Paul did not call this girl out right away. Perhaps he may not have discerned this initially. The passage informs us that he exorcised this girl after she followed them "many days." "Then Paul, being sorely annoyed *and* worn out turned and said to the spirit within her, I charge you in the name of Jesus Christ to come out of her!"- Clearly, this girl was harassing Paul, and it got on his nerves. However, the point here is that this girl practiced advanced stages of divination to the point where she was now possessed by a demon that gave her this information about these two missionaries.

Demons can transfer information from the supernatural to the natural realm, but they need a vessel or a "medium" to channel the information. A *medium* is a person that is sensitive to the subtle realities of the cosmos, and therefore is particularly capable of communicating with spirit entities.[49] Mediums are very receptive to the higher vibrations of the spirit world. This *vibration* phenomenon was covered by the film and book titled *The Secret*. As a true prophet is the mouthpiece for God's prophetic revelation, so are mediums the mouthpiece for the spirits that speak through them.[50] This is particularly disconcerting when we see that the Scriptures inform us: "But the Spirit explicitly says that in later times some will fall away from the faith, paying attention to deceitful spirits and doctrines of demons, by means of the hypocrisy of liars seared in their own conscience as with a branding iron..." (1 Tim.4:1-2, NASB).

Of particular interest to this aspect of our study is what Timothy calls "deceitful (seducing) spirits, and doctrines of demons." In order for a false prophet to receive doctrine from a demon, they must be in connection with these spirit entities, thus fulfilling the role of a medium through which the demon needs to channel its messages. Here is what the Scriptures have to say about mediums: "Do not turn to mediums or seek out spiritists, for you will be defiled by them. I am the LORD your God" (Lev.19:31). Note that the Lord does not say, "might be or could be defiled." He says explicitly that "you *will be* defiled by them."

False prophets that we see today who call out people's phone numbers, addresses, Social Security numbers, or know other hidden things about individuals that they have never met can only do this by one of three ways:1) They have done advanced research on individuals attending the service or conference from a registration list, or social media, or been given the information by church staff that host them. To this there is nothing supernatural. This is just a plain con game. 2) The false prophets have learned sensory or perception techniques from the various forms of divination. But it is not the author's assertion that false prophets are using divination, the Bible makes this claim. Such dabbling in divination serves as a gateway to demonic influence and even possession. Remember, a false prophet has not been sent by God, even though they speak in God's name. 3) The false prophet is under the influence of or possessed by a demonic spirit and therefore possesses various levels of supernatural enablement, perception, and sensitivities and even miracle-working faculties.

Since these demons are *seducing spirits*, they have deceived false prophets into believing that they are under the unction of the Holy Spirit. Again, this is the whole premise behind *Counterfeit Charisma,* which in short is counterfeit gifts with the kingdom of darkness power behind them. The *modus operandi* of Satan has always been to steal, kill, and destroy (John 10:10). Therefore, Satan transforms himself into an angel of light to deceive people into believing that they are in the presence of God, when in fact it is Lucifer, or other wicked principalities and powers. These prophets believe that their gifts and powers are legitimate, when in reality they are counterfeit. This is why John states, "Dear friends, do not believe every spirit, but test the spirits to see whether they are from God, because many false prophets have gone out into the world" (1 John 4:1). Notice the term "spirit(s)" is interchangeable with "false prophets," thus testifying to the supernatural, demonic aspect of false prophets. However, all false prophets do not flow in the supernatural; some are ordained ministers that teach in seminaries that deny foundational tenets of Christian doctrine such as the bodily incarnation of the Lord, which was a common Gnostic heresy of John's day. Today, many liberal scholars deny the resurrection and virgin birth of Jesus. These also qualify as false teachers and prophets.

THE LYING SPIRITS

> And he said, I saw all Israel scattered upon the hills, as sheep that have not a shepherd: and the LORD said, These have no master: let them return every man to his house in peace.
>
> 1 Kings 22:17, KJV

Ahab, King of Israel, is probably best known as a spineless ruler whose wicked wife Jezebel controlled him. During these times, kings consulted with their prophets before making important decisions or particularly before going to war. Ahab reluctantly called for Micaiah, a true prophet of the Lord, to see what the Lord had to say about the outcome of an attack on Syria. The prophet then related to Ahab a vision that the Lord had given him. Then Micaiah answered, "I saw all Israel scattered on the hills like sheep without a shepherd, and the LORD said, 'These people have no master. Let each one go home in peace'" (1 Kings 22:17). This indicated that Ahab would be killed and his armies dispersed. After this, the fearless prophet spoke up again,

> *At one school of prophets, students learned how to tune into certain musical notes (vibrations) through meditation. During these exercises the student's sensitivity would be heightened to be able to tap into the metaphysical.*

but this time, he told the king of another prophetic vision that he had. The prophet revealed how Ahab was going to be persuaded to fight a losing battle with the Syrians. To examine this very intriguing account, we must refer to 1 Kings 22, verses 20 through 23:

> Then *Micaiah* said, "Therefore hear the word of the LORD: I saw the LORD sitting on His throne, and all the hosts of heaven standing by, on His right hand and on His left. And the LORD said, 'Who will persuade Ahab to go up, that he may fall at Ramoth Gilead?' So one spoke in this manner, and another spoke in that manner. Then a spirit came forward and stood before the LORD, and said, 'I will persuade him.' The LORD said to him, 'In what way?' So he said, 'I will go out and be a lying spirit in the mouth of all his prophets.' And the LORD said, 'You shall persuade *him,* and also prevail. Go out and do so.' Therefore look! The LORD has put a lying spirit in the mouth of all these prophets of yours, and the LORD has declared disaster against you."
>
> 1 Kings 22:19-23, NKJV

Here, the Scriptures give us an account of a *lying spirit* at work. This spirit had the power to influence the thoughts, motivations, and words of Ahab's prophets. It was by the deceptive words of these false prophets that Ahab was convinced to fight against Syria. Having his pride swollen by their lying predictions, Ahab was lured into the battle that would cost him his life. Though he despised Micaiah's prophecy, Ahab still took precautions to protect himself by not wearing his royal clothes into battle but instead, wore a disguise. But by God's providence, a random arrow struck Ahab in the crease of his armor and killed him, just as Micaiah prophesied.

Before leaving for battle, Ahab had ordered that Micaiah be locked up until Ahab returned. Undoubtedly, Ahab would have killed Micaiah if he *had* returned. However, listen to the bold statement that Micaiah made as he was carted off to jail: But Micaiah said, "If you ever return in peace, the LORD has not spoken by me." And he said, "Take heed, all you people" (1 Kings 22:28, NKJV)!

Micaiah punctuated his prophecy by saying, "Let everybody here understand what I just prophesied. If the king comes back here alive, everyone will know the Lord has not spoken to me and I am a false prophet!" A true prophet can put their life and reputation on the line and not worry about trying to convince anyone of their veracity or be concerned about who does or doesn't like it.

THE METAPHYSICAL—GATEWAY TO THE DEMONIC

Not long ago, a ministerial associate, whom I will call Walter, and I had a conversation about a certain prophet that ran a school of prophets who incorporated some of the metaphysical arts into his curriculum to enhance his students' prophetic abilities. One of the definitions for *Metaphysical* means: *beyond the physical or material; incorporeal, supernatural or transcendental.*[51] Walter said that this prophet stated that "he looked for students that had an innate sensitivity to the metaphysical." During the training at this school of prophets, he would teach his students how to tune into certain musical notes (vibrations) through meditation. During these exercises, the students sensitivity would be heightened to be able to tune in to the metaphysical, which enabled them to pull messages and information out of the air. I was completely blown away when he was sharing this with me.

Similarly, on another website, a prophet who also has a school of prophets was teaching "25 signs that you have been called to be a prophet." One of the signs was that prophets "flow," meaning that "a prophet needs music or noise to flow." He went on to say, "You want to hear music and you want to hear messages." Then he lied and said, "Every prophet in the Old Testament, you hear them say, 'I want to prophesy, bring me the musicians to come here so they can play for me.'" Of course he didn't give any Scriptural reference for this. Why? Because there are none! Nowhere in the Bible does a prophet call for singers to sing, or musicians to play, so the prophet could give a prophecy. Of course music does play an important role in worship (Col. 3:16), and musical sounds even in war (Jos. 6:20, 2 Chron. 20:21, Ps. 150), but nowhere in the Bible is there anything about a prophet requiring music in order to prophesy.

Walter's description of what was taught at this particular school of prophets pertaining to tuning in to certain notes to heighten the prophets' sensitivity is similar, but not identical, to practices found in mystical religions and new age practices where chants like the "Om" or "Aum" (like the humming monotone note Buddhist monks make) are found.

Here is what is said about the Om:

> Om is a sacred sound of the divine. It is a mysterious expression of the infinity, timelessness, eternity and wisdom. Om (vibrations of the om) is our true nature, our higher self, the core of our inner being. As we all are vibrations on a micro level, so when we chant Om, again and again, we create its pure vibrations in our body. We become in tune with the vibrations of the Om and we become one with the Om. Om chanting connects us to all that is living, from beings to nature, to the Universe.[52]

In many of these mystical practices and religions, the universe is given divine faculties. You will hear people say, "The universe will bless you." What the Om does is connect you with the universe through Om vibration. This is where these long notes come in. Notice that in these prophetic meetings, there is always softly playing in the background not just any music, but prolonged soft notes where the prophet often sings. These are not melodic sounds, but rather meditative sounds. Admittedly, the point I am making here is inconclusive. However, once you strip away the Buddhist or new age terminology and just focus on the technique itself, you will find the similarities striking.

Walter went on to say that he actually saw the prophet use this technique during a church service, but he noticed that after the prophet called out some numbers (maybe someone's address or phone number) there was nothing that followed behind it. Nothing specific or profoundly prophetic, but after the numbers were called out, there were no more prophetic details. Though people were amazed with the numbers trick, Walter knew that this was not legitimate prophecy.

Walter went on to tell of another minister that he knew who also went to this school. He too claimed that he learned how to meditate on musical notes and colors to be able to tune into the elemental vibrations which allow him to tap into deeper realms of knowledge that are of a divination nature. According to Walter, these "prophets" were not learning from the Bible or being taught Christian doctrine, but were being trained in the metaphysical. Once this preacher mastered the technique, he used it when he preached, and it was very effective on the people. But something must have happened, because he started getting convicted once he realized that what he was doing was not inspired by the Holy Spirit, but was practicing divination to raise offerings. He said other preachers were blowing up his phone for him to come minister at their churches because of his abilities. Divination passed off as prophecy brings in the big bucks. Remember what the Scriptures said? "…Her priests instruct for a price. And her prophets divine for money…" (Micah 3:11, NASB).

Finally, Walter said that a lot of these people that attended this particular school of prophets have the wrong motives, because they want to learn how to amaze people with divination while they pass it off as the movement of the Holy Spirit. When you tap into the metaphysical, you are able to hear "those familiar spirits" call out names and numbers. These are the same spirits that spiritists and soothsayers tap into that enable them to transfer information about others to the prophet.

In a newsletter titled *Altered States*, the following is stated: "Sound is also a vibration and so are thoughts. Everything that manifests itself in your life is there because it matches the vibration from your thoughts."[53] From this occultic information, also taught heavily in the book and movie *The Secret*, you will see that what Walter was describing at this particular school of prophets and what the cultist in this newsletter is saying are very similar. However, there is one distinction that must be pointed out, and that is, the proponents of this philosophy think they are tuning into the vibrations of the universe, but they are really tapping into the deceptive powers of demons. Evil spirits want to deceive people into thinking that they are worshiping anything other than a demon. They don't care if you think you are receiving a message from God when it's really from them.

JANNES AND JAMBRES

No study concerning the deceptive powers of hell would be complete without interjecting two names, Jannes and Jambres, into the discussion. These individuals appear in 2 Timothy 3. Though they remain somewhat of an enigma, they are an integral part of this aspect of our study. Our text reads:

> These teachers oppose the truth just as Jannes and Jambres opposed Moses. They have depraved minds and a counterfeit faith. But they won't get away with this for long. Someday everyone will recognize what fools they are, just as with Jannes and Jambres.
>
> 2 Timothy 3:8-9, NLT

It is noteworthy that Paul associates false teachers and their counterfeit faith with *Jannes and Jambres*. Though there is no mention of either of these two in the *Pentateuch* (the first five books of the Old Testament, ascribed to Moses), clearly Paul identifies them as the ones that opposed Moses. Their names come to us by Jewish, Christian, and Pagan literature as two of Pharaoh's magicians that tried to demonstrate that they could perform miracles just as effectively as Moses.[54] Examining the actions of these two will help us understand the extent of powers behind these and other *miracle-working* false prophets.

In Exodus 7, we find the first contest between a real prophet and false prophets that reveals some astonishing facts:

> So Moses and Aaron went to Pharaoh and did just as the LORD commanded. Aaron threw his staff down in front of Pharaoh and his officials, and it became a snake. Pharaoh then summoned wise men and sorcerers, and the Egyptian magicians also did the same things by their secret arts: Each one threw down his staff and it became a snake. But Aaron's staff swallowed up their staffs. Yet Pharaoh's heart became hard and he would not listen to them, just as the LORD had said.
>
> Exodus 7:10-13

This text is fascinating in that it reveals the miracles performed by emissaries of two different spiritual kingdoms: the kingdom of light, and the kingdom of darkness. An inanimate piece of wood becoming a reptile reveals a power source far beyond mere human capability. Whereas we know Yahweh was the source of Moses' power, we must also concede that the source of power behind Jannes and Jambres was Satan. Though some may argue that Jannes and Jambres' were false miracles or lying wonders, that does not mitigate the fact that their staffs became snakes as well. Further proof of a legitimate supernatural event is the fact that Aaron's snake *swallowed* the magicians' snakes. The principal point of this passage is that counterfeit power, although

real power, is not lasting power.[55] Secondly, God was the miracle worker working through Moses and Aaron, which was quite a different case
than Jannes and Jambres performing their miracle through the use of
"secret arts." Nevertheless, though inferior and counterfeit, the point is
that they too turned a piece of wood into a snake.

These "secret arts" were the subject of interest in the book of Acts,
where believers at Ephesus turned over their "curious arts" books and
materials and burned them, after the news of a demon-possessed man
beating Sceva and his sons for trying to cast out a demon in the name
of Jesus, as Paul preached, spread throughout the region. The demon's
response in this somewhat humorous incident was, "Jesus I know, and
Paul I know, but who are you?" The text states that many of the believers at Ephesus used "curious arts." This literature falls under the
general subject of divinatory literature passed down through the centuries. Whether called *curious* or *secret* arts, these practices are forbidden
in the Scriptures but are practiced in various forms throughout all
cultures in all ages (ref. Acts 19:13-20).

It is interesting that besides duplicating the rod-into-snake miracle,
Jannes and Jambres also duplicated the first two of the ten plagues
sent against the Egyptians: turning water into blood, and the plague
of the frogs (Ex 7:22, 8:7). However, they could not proceed further.
Exodus 8:18-19 reads,

> But when the magicians tried to produce gnats by their
> secret arts, they could not. Since the gnats were on peo-
> ple and animals everywhere, the magicians said to Pha-
> raoh, "This is the finger of God." But Pharaoh's heart
> was hard and he would not listen, just as the LORD had
> said.   Exodus 8:18-19

From this passage we see that the magicians were in over their heads
with trying to duplicate this plague. Much discussion among scholars

and expositors has occurred as to the reason why this was so. One school of thought is that the gnats were too small a creature to be manipulated and reproduced by the magicians. But this seems implausible. A more palatable explanation is that the gnats came from the dust of the earth. However, the Egyptian magicians' "power source" of their "secret arts" was empowered by the Nile. Therefore, the magicians were completely out of their element. Jehovah is the God of all creation. Jannes and Jambres were not able to reproduce the plague, because the power of their gods was limited.[56]

All of this is important to our study, because, even if a contemporary false prophet possesses miracle-working faculties, their power, though amazing and even quite convincing, will still be limited, because the source of their enablement is not God. Therefore, like Jannes and Jambres, they will only be able to go so far. This is why Jesus' miracles were such a powerful testimony as to who He was. The miracles that He performed were way beyond what anyone had ever done or could ever do. For example, Jesus' healing of the man born blind was a miracle that was completely off the charts. Here is what they said, "Since the beginning of time it has never been heard that anyone opened the eyes of a person born blind. If this man were not from God, He could do nothing" (John 9:32-33, NASB). The Lord asked Abraham "is there anything too hard for God?" (Gen. 18:14). With God, there are no limits. The power source the false prophets tap into, which they think is God, is not; that power source is limited.

Without a doubt, a false prophet will defend this practice to the end because they are blinded by greedy ambition and Satan's subterfuge. It is true, some of these false prophets do have power. There is no question about that. However, while the power that they do have does come from a "spirit," it is not the Holy Spirit. Some of them know in the depths of their heart that they are false, while others are deceived and will live out their lives under this great deception, only to come to

> *Though they use the same divination techniques, the real difference between psychics and false prophets, is that the false prophet claims to be a Christian and uses the Bible to justify their practices.*

Judgment Day to find out that they were false. Surely they will claim, "Lord, Lord, have we not prophesied in your name, and in your name cast out devils, and in your name performed miracles?" But Jesus will reply," I never knew you, depart from me ye that work iniquity" (ref. Matt.7:21-23). I can think of no greater horror than standing before the Lord on Judgment Day, thinking that you were in relationship with Him and finding out that He never knew you, even though, you prophesied, cast out devils, and did miracles in His name. Unfortunately, many people that end up in hell will have gone there passing right through the doors of the local church.

THE FORENSIC PINPOINT LEVEL OF PROPHECY

Certain schools of the prophets teach what is called *Forensic Pinpoint Level of Prophecy*, which enables prophets to pull names and telephone numbers "out of the air," or as others say it, hear this information in the spirit, or see it with your "spiritual eye." Though fascinating, it's not of God. It is interesting that a seemingly technical name has been given to a deceptive practice. Previously, we stated that there are only three ways to know someone's personal information like names, addresses, and telephone numbers: advanced research, the information is provided to the prophet, or they are in communion with wicked spirit entities such as demons. The last is the most serious, because it is a direct pipeline to the kingdom of darkness. The last is the category where we find forensic pinpoint level of prophecy. Forensic pinpoint level of prophecy amazes people all over the world, because a complete stranger is able to tell you information about yourself that they couldn't possibly know, but they do it under the guise of legitimate prophecy.

In this obscure divination practice, it is claimed that God imparts people's names, telephone numbers, addresses, or other tidbits of personal information to prophets that have learned how to use this technique to gain access to this information. Make no mistake about it, this is truly *supernatural*, but it is not of God. It is important to understand that the practice of pulling this information out of the air, seeing inside someone's house, knowing where someone works, or calling out children's names and birthdays is nothing more than what psychics and mediums have done since the beginning of time. Obtaining this information through the use of spirits is an old phenomenon, and is the very reason why God said that he drove out the nations before Israel (see Deut. 18:9-13).

I once heard the testimony of a woman that said this prophet told her what her house looked like, the color of her door, what it looked like on the inside, and so on. Each time she recounted what the prophet told her, she exclaimed, "This had to be God." Why? Because the prophet was "accurate." However, this is the same thing the people said of Simon Magus, that he was "the great power of God." This is exactly what Satan wants people to believe.

In the realm of psychic ability, seeing distant places where the psychic or false prophet has never been is known as "remote viewing." Clairvoyants have been doing this for years. They can see distant places and relate accurate details without actually going there. Surprisingly, governmental entities like the military and CIA have trained individuals in using this technique,[57] although it has been found to be unreliable. Law enforcement agencies have consulted psychics in order to solve crimes, particularly murders. You can go on any number of psychic websites and see remote viewing ability offered as a psychic service. Psychic websites typically market their services by also promoting how "accurate" their psychics are.

The false prophet to whom I was speaking of teaches others how to receive the ability to operate in forensic pinpoint level of prophecy. He stated that in order to receive this prophetic gift, you must be under and connect with someone that currently operates in that gift. Then he clarified what he meant by *connect*, which was sowing a seed (or giving money). Only then could that prophetic ability in turn be imparted or transferred to the one who gives money to the false prophet. Once again, it was all about the money. The fact that one must go to a specific individual or a certain school to receive this ability, is a dead give a way that this is divination, not divine. However, this is what the Scriptures say about the distribution of Spiritual gifts: "It is the one and only Spirit who distributes all these gifts. He alone decides which gift each person should have" (1 Cor. 12:11, NLT).

After this the false prophet started teaching on developing your "third eye" so that you can see into the spirit realm. Again, psychics also refer to their ability as a "third eye" too. Though they use the same divination techniques, the real difference between a psychic and a false prophet is that the false prophet claims to be a Christian and uses the Bible to justify their practices. They typically mix mysticism and divination with tenets of Christian doctrine to create the false doctrines found in many churches today. For example, the false prophet started to teach some very bizarre things, like Adam and Eve were physically blind but could see only through their third eye. He referenced Genesis, where it says, "… And when the woman saw that the tree *was* good for food, and that it *was* pleasant to the eyes, and a tree to be desired to make *one* wise…" (Gen. 3:6, KJV). From that the false prophet stated that this proves that Eve was using her "spiritual eye," because you cannot see something that can make you "wise" with the natural eyes. Of course, this is a wildly heretical position and total misuse of the Scriptures. He said that only after Adam and Eve sinned did they begin to see through their "physical eyes." So I assume we are to understand that they had physical eyes all the time, but just weren't using them? Again, ridiculous!

> *When people are out of the will of God whether it is because of sin, disobedience or whatever reason, seeking out a prophet is a waste of time... if God is your problem, a word from a prophet will not deliver you*

In another one of his teachings, the false prophet went on to speak about how the prophet Daniel (of the Old Testament) appeared to him in a dream and began to teach him more about the use of the "third eye." This same prophet also claims to have gone back in time to the 1800s, when he started prophesying to a woman about her ancestors from Russia. The false prophet was able to give names and dates about her family members which had been dead for over a hundred years. The woman and the congregation were totally amazed. In regards to the woman's family, either he was able to obtain some historical information about this woman's relatives, or he was consulting with a familiar spirit, or was practicing necromancy, the divination where mediums consult with the dead. Calling what amounts to necromancy "pinpoint forensic prophecy" attempts to give legitimacy to a clearly forbidden practice.

THE WITCH OF EN DOR

> *And the person who turns to mediums and familiar spirits, to prostitute himself with them, I will set My face against that person and cut him off from his people. Leviticus 20:6, NKJV*

In 1 Samuel 28, we find a very strange account of the "Witch of En Dor" or, more properly, the "Medium of En Dor." This is the person that King Saul consulted with to bring up the prophet Samuel from the dead in order to inquire about what the outcome of the battle with the Philistines would be. Saul complained that since the Lord would not answer him through a prophet or dreams, he had no choice but to seek the assistance of a necromancer (one who consults with the dead).

> Saul then said to his attendants, "Find me a woman who is a medium, so I may go and inquire of her." "There is one in Endor," they said. Then the woman asked, "Whom shall I bring up for you?" "Bring up Samuel," he said. When the woman saw Samuel, she cried out at the top of her voice and said to Saul, "Why have you deceived me? You are Saul!" The king said to her, "Don't be afraid. What do you see?" The woman said, "I see a ghostly figure coming up out of the earth." "What does he look like?" he asked. "An old man wearing a robe is coming up," she said. Then Saul knew it was Samuel, and he bowed down and prostrated himself with his face to the ground. Samuel said to Saul, "Why have you disturbed me by bringing me up?" "I am in great distress," Saul said. "The Philistines are fighting against me, and God has departed from me. He no longer answers me, either by prophets or by dreams. So I have called on you to tell me what to do."
>
> 1 Samuel 28:7, 11-15

Though this account has been the subject of great debate followed by various interpretations, the fact remains that a medium that consults with "familiar spirits" was able to call up Samuel's spirit from the dead, allowing King Saul to consult with him. Though this defies human reasoning, these powers—though wicked—are real, and thus invoke judgment from the Lord of those that consult with anyone that uses this form of divination (Lev.20:6, NKJV).

As I covered earlier, the false prophet that has the school of prophets training other prophets in the use of pinpoint forensic prophecy states in one of his training sessions that he consults with "Daniel the prophet in the Bible." Brothers and sisters, as we are all quite aware, Daniel has been dead for thousands of years. In an attempt to sound deep and give himself authority, this deceiver confesses from his own mouth that he consults with a dead prophet. God calls these damnable practices, heretical doctrines, and philosophies abominations, yet they are being practiced in the Church as Holy Spirit-inspired prophecy. The fact that this prophet openly flaunts that he communicates with dead folk indicates that he is banking on one of two things: 1) people will be impressed with his range of supernatural ability, or 2) people are ignorant to the prohibitions against such practices explicitly delineated in Scripture.

Since Saul consulted with the witch or medium, he was judged:

> The battle became fierce against Saul. The archers hit him, and he was wounded by the archers. Then Saul said to his armor bearer, "Draw your sword, and thrust me through with it, lest these uncircumcised men come and abuse me." But his armor bearer would not, for he was greatly afraid. Therefore Saul took a sword and fell on it…So Saul died for his unfaithfulness which he had committed against the LORD, because he did not keep the word of the LORD, and also because he consulted a medium for guidance. But *he* did not inquire of the LORD; therefore He killed him, and turned the kingdom over to David the son of Jesse.
>
> 1 Chronicles 10:3-4, 13-14, NKJV

The tragic end of King Saul was that he died in defeat and disgrace. Not only did he have to see his three sons, including Jonathan, die, but his disgrace was punctuated by his own suicide. God took Saul's kingdom because he disobeyed His command, but He killed him for consulting a medium for guidance.

There is an important point that we must emphasize before we conclude this discussion. Saul was out of the will of God so he could no longer hear from God. In a nutshell, that was Saul's problem. His disobedience cut him off from God. When people are out of the will of God whether it is because of sin, disobedience or whatever reason, seeking out a prophet to hear a prophetic word is a waste of time. If Satan is your problem, you can go to God for help. But, if God is your problem, a word from a false prophet will not deliver you.

CHAPTER EIGHT

EMPOWERED TO DECEIVE

THE ANTI-ANOINTING

In the previous chapters we have covered how there are three ways that false prophets can prophesy and know information about people they have never met. 1) They have done advance research on individuals attending the service or conference from a registration list or social media, or have been provided the information by host church staff or others. 2) The false prophets practice metaphysical techniques from the various forms of divination. 3) The false prophets are under the influence of, in connection with, or even possessed by, a demonic spirit that gives them access to knowledge, whether it's doctrine or secret things about others, or telling the future.

In some cases, false prophets might even possess miracle-working faculties which, according to the Scriptures, can be so amazing that even the very elect would be deceived (Matt. 24:24). However, even if they have this power, such as in the case with *Jannes and Jambres*, their power, though impressive, is still limited. The fact that it is limited is important, because that means their source (Satan) is also limited.

Supernatural events that occur in the natural realm (in the broad sense, miracles) come from either God's or Satan's power. There is no in between. With some commentators, whether or not Satan can produce a *legitimate* miracle is the subject of ongoing debate. However, a clear distinction can be made between the two. Godly miracles are always in perfect conformity with His righteousness and holiness, purpose, plan, and will, and always bring glory to God. On the other hand, Satan's miracles are for the purposes of deception, to bring glory to himself in order to move people away from God, by appealing to man's fallen nature, through the lust of the flesh, the lust of the eye, and the pride of life (more on this in the following chapter). However, as we discussed concerning Moses and Aaron versus Jannes and Jambres, both sides threw down wooden rods that became serpents. This is important for this aspect of our study, because there is another word for "power" that we use today called the *anointing*.

THE ANOINTING

Since the emergence of the contemporary Pentecostal movement of the early 1900s, much has been made of the Holy Spirit's work in the Church. Considerable attention has been focused on the believer being *anointed* with spiritual gifts and enablements for Christian lifestyle and service. Though the subject of *the Anointing* is a bit overrated in some circles, this does not mitigate its validity. There are more than one hundred sixty references in both Old and New Testaments where various forms of the word *anointing* are found. Being anointed is an undeniable aspect of a dynamic relationship with the Lord. Since Jesus is the Christ, or *the anointed one*, Christians inevitably share in His anointing.

One of the most widely referenced texts concerning the anointing is found in Luke 4:18. In this text, the Lord is at the synagogue in Nazareth when He begins to read from the prophet Isaiah. The passage says:

> The Spirit of the Lord is upon me, because he hath anointed me to preach the gospel to the poor; he hath sent me to heal the brokenhearted, to preach deliverance to the captives, and recovering of sight to the blind, to set at liberty them that are bruised.
>
> Luke 4:18, KJV

In this passage, as well as Acts 10:38 (Jesus anointed with the Holy Spirit and power....), it is clear that the anointing is in reference to the empowerment of the Holy Spirit. Another reference to the anointing that has been popularized is also found in Isaiah 10:27. In this passage, Isaiah speaks of the anointing destroying yokes of bondage. In the Psalms, God speaks of His *anointed ones*, such as His prophets (Psalms105:15).The term *anointing* can also be used synonymously for the Holy Spirit (1 John 2:27).

Primarily the word translated as *anoint* in English comes from Hebrew words like *shah,*[58] *sûk,*[59] and several Greek words like *aleiphō,*[60] *myrizō,*[61] *epichriō,*[62] and *chriō,*[63] all having similar meanings, such as to oil, to pour, to smear. With all these words, the basic idea is *to rub or smear onto an object or an individual.* Although olive oil was primarily used to anoint something, other substances were also used. For example, when the Lord healed the blind man in John 9:6, it is said that the Lord *anointed* the blind man's eyes with the spittle clay. In this passage, *anointed* meant the Lord actually smeared the clay on the man's eyes.

The anointing was often transferable. Elijah transferred a double portion of his Spirit (*his anointing*) to Elisha through his mantle (2 Kings 2:9-15).Moses transferred the Spirit of wisdom to Joshua by laying hands upon him (Deut. 34:9). The woman with the issue of blood received healing of her infirmity when she, by faith, touched him (Luke 8:43-48).God used the Apostle Paul to touch handkerchiefs and aprons of the sick and demon-possessed. The anointing in Paul was transferred to these handkerchiefs and aprons. Those who then touched these items were miraculously healed (Acts 19:11-12). (Unfortunately, some ministers today sell handkerchiefs that are supposed to have healing power too—what a joke.)

To get a greater insight into the anointing, let's look again to the Lord. When we think of the many alternate names, attributed to Jesus, there is a common misconception about one of his primary titles. I am referring to the word *Christ.* Many people treat *Christ* as if it were Jesus' last name. Though in some passages the term is used as a proper name, primarily it is a title. The word *Christ* comes from the Greek word

Christos,[64] which means *"Anointed." Christos* is equivalent to the Hebrew word *māshîah,*[65] translated to *Messiah,* which means *"the Anointed One."*

In the early days of the Church there was much persecution of those who were part of what was referred to as *"the Way."* The expression *"the Way"* implied someone who was characterized by a course of conduct, or a way of thinking. In this case, belief in Christ was the object of this *New Way* (Acts 9:2 19:23). At this juncture in Church history, there was no specific term that designated the followers of Christ. However, approximately nine years after the resurrection of Christ, in Antioch those who were followers of Jesus Christ were called *Christians* for the first time. Although this name was probably applied to the believers as more of a term for identification purposes, the truth is that the term was most appropriate.

Since Christ was the *Anointed One,* those who trusted Him as their Lord shared in his anointing. Therefore, it was quite fitting that they were called *Christians.* On the Day of Pentecost, this anointing was made available to all believers. Wherefore, the Scriptures declare, *"If any man have not the Spirit of Christ, he is none of his"* (Rom. 8:9b). All true Christians share in Christ's Spirit and his anointing. In the book of 1 John, the apostle says: *"But the anointing which ye have received of him abideth in you..."* (1 John 2:27). Who then abides in the Christian? Christ Himself. As Jesus clearly declares in St. John, *Abide in me, and I in you. As the branch cannot bear fruit of itself, except it abide in the vine; no more can ye, except ye abide in me* (John 15:4).

Another word used in place of the term *anointing* is the word *unction.* Whereas the word *anointing* is used three times in the New Testament, the word *unction* is used only once. The word *unction* comes from the Greek word *chrisma,* which means an unguent, a smearing, or the endowment of the Holy Spirit.[66] The words *chrisma* and *charisma* are very similar, but with these distinctions: *chrisma* speaks of the power or the anointing itself. *Charisma* speaks of the *gifts, e.g., tongues, prophecy,* through which the anointing operates.

THE DISTRIBUTION OF THE ANOINTING

In the 133rd Psalm, David, speaking of brethren who dwell in unity, says: *"It is like the precious ointment upon the head, that ran down upon the beard, even Aaron's beard: that went down to the skirts of his garments"*(Psalms 133:2). Though the word *ointment* is used in this Psalm, it is in reference to the Holy *anointing oil,* referred to several times in both Exodus and Leviticus. According to the Law, Moses was to take the anointing oil and apply it to Aaron's head, then his garments. The same process was repeated on Aaron's sons and then their garments (Lev. 8:30). The anointing of Aaron's head and garments, and his sons' heads and garments, respectively, symbolically represents a succession in the flow of the anointing. Likewise, there is a similar type of order in the Church. As Paul states, *"And he is before all things, and by him all things consist. And he is the head of the body, the church...that in all things he might have the preeminence"*(Col. 1:17-18). Christ, *the anointed one,* is the *head* of the body, the *Church.* The head was first anointed, and from the head the anointing flows downward to the rest of the body. Just as it is stated in 1 John 2:27, it is from Christ, the Head of the Body, that we receive our anointing. It is important to realize the anointing was given to the Body, so that all men could profit withal (1 Cor. 12:7). These gifts and enablements were never meant to be exploited for personal gain. Since people are all limited, spiritual gifts compensate for our weaknesses and inabilities. These gifts and enablements were never meant to be a means within themselves, nor were they to be esteemed as the objects of our salvation. We are not saved *because* we have gifts. But since we are saved, *we have* spiritual gifts, which are blessings and benefits of salvation (Rom.12:3-8).

Examining the anointing was necessary in order for us to understand how Satan uses his *counterfeit* anointing. Some of the same principles that we find in the allocation of God's anointing are similar to how Satan distributes his *anti-anointing.* If it seems strange that the devil would try to copy some of God's methods, it shouldn't. Why? The answer to this question can be found in Satan's desire to be like God. In Isaiah 14:14 we get a glimpse of the Devil's mindset. The prophet, revealing Satan's wicked sentiments, says: *"I will ascend above the heights of the clouds; I will be like the most High."* It has always been Satan's desire to be like God, especially in the sense of receiving worship as the Supreme Being. Part of his whole scheme is to wield his powers of deception and persuasion to cause men to worship him. It should always be remembered that though the Devil comes to steal, kill, and destroy, he accomplishes this by deception. The Devil never makes his intentions obvious. Although he is eternally reprobate and condemned, nevertheless he is a formidable foe, in both the heavenly and earthly realms.

THE ANOINTED CHERUBIM

In Ezekiel 28, we find a very interesting passage of Scripture, which is two-fold as it relates to the character depicted in the text. The passage says:

> Son of man, take up a lamentation over the king of Tyre and say to him, 'Thus says the Lord GOD, "You had the seal of perfection, Full of wisdom and perfect in beauty." You were in Eden, the garden of God; Every precious stone was your covering: The ruby, the topaz and the diamond; The beryl, the onyx and the jasper; The lapis lazuli, the turquoise and the emerald; And the gold, the workmanship of your settings and sockets, Was in you. On the day that you were created They were prepared. "You were **the anointed cherub** who covers, And I placed you *there*. You were on the holy mountain of God; You walked in the midst of the stones of fire. "You were blameless in your ways From the day you were created Until unrighteousness was found in you." By the abundance of your trade You were internally filled with violence, And

you sinned; Therefore I have cast you as profane From the mountain of God. And I have destroyed you, O covering cherub, From the midst of the stones of fire.

Ezekiel 28:12-16, NASB

In Ezekiel 27, the prophet is told to take up a lamentation against the city of Tyre, a port of the Phoenicians that was twenty-five miles south of Sidon and fifteen miles north of the Lebanese border with Israel.[67] However, in the 28th chapter, the attention turns to the King of Tyre, whom historians believed to be *Ethbaal II* (585–573 B.C.).[68] Ethbaal II was a very prideful ruler. In verses 2 and 3 of the 28th chapter, God begins to state His case against the prideful monarch by recalling the king's prideful assertions: The king boasted "...*I am a God, I sit in the seat of God....*" Remarkably, this is the same language that the anti-christ will use (see 2 Thes. 2:4).

The context of Ezekiel 27 and 28 is a clear case of God's pronouncement of judgment against this wicked city and its arrogant king. However, there seem to be dual textual focuses which extend beyond the borders and era of the ancient city. Depending upon which commentaries you read, you'll find different opinions on who's actually the focus of this text. Some commentators claim the king of Tyre is the only personage referred to here. Others say the text focuses in on Satan prior to his heavenly rebellion. I believe this prophecy is at least two-fold in that it depicts both the ancient king and the Devil. Though there may be some similarities between both the king of Tyre and Satan, there are certain aspects of this text that clearly allude to Lucifer.

First of all, Ezekiel describes this person as being: "*Sealed up the sum of wisdom, and perfect in beauty.*" Although Ethbaal II, king of Tyre, may have been both brilliant and attractive, nevertheless, he was fallible, having imperfections and blemishes just like any other person. Therefore, this description could not be applied to him. Secondly, it is said, *Thou hast been in Eden the garden of God.* This statement can only be applied to no other personage than Satan. There was no one alive in Ezekiel's day that could have been in the *Garden of Eden*. It is an unequivocal, Biblical fact that Adam and Eve were the last and only people ever to set foot in the garden.

Thirdly, the person referred to in this text is called the *"Anointed Cherub that Covereth."* What is a *cherub*? The *cherub*, or *cherubim*, seems to be a high-ranking order of angelic being. Though the word *cherubim* has an uncertain derivation, the term is found only once in the New Testament, but over ninety times in the Old Testament. These mysterious beings, also referred to as *"The Living Creatures,"* seem to function in the following three ways: (1) As guardians. (2) As functionaries in the immediate presence of God. (3) And they are associated with God's throne and His holiness. Though descriptions of their appearance are obscure (two faces and two wings or four faces and four wings), they were hardly human beings like Ethbaal II.

Since the term *cherubim* is used in reference to the king of Tyre, this prophecy is obviously looking beyond the human king of Tyre, to Satan himself. As a cherubim, Satan's angelic name was *Lucifer*, which means *The Morning Star*. Isaiah 14:12, is the only passage in the *Authorized Version* of the Bible where this name is found. This is the same chapter where the prophet records Satan's five infamous *"I will"* statements which lead to his fall from heaven (Isa. 14:12-15). The prophet Ezekiel's account also describes him as *"the anointed cherub that covereth."* Though there is some debate over what this means, Exodus 25:20 could give some insight into this mystery.

In this text we find God's instructions to Moses on how to construct the *Ark of the Covenant*. The Ark of the Covenant was the most sacred object found in Israel's pre-exilic sanctuary. The Ark was a type of chest that was made of choice shittim wood and overlaid with pure gold. Situated on the ark was the lid that fit over its top. Configured upon the lid was the golden *Mercy Seat*. The Mercy Seat, which was also the Throne of God, was the place for propitiatory atonement.

Affixed on either side of the Mercy Seat were the golden cherubims.

Concerning the cherubims, Exodus 25:20 says: "And the cherubims shall stretch forth their wings on high, *covering* the mercy seat with their wings, and their faces shall look one to another; towards the mercy seat shall their faces be."In Hebrews 8:5, the writer tells us that Israel's earthly tabernacle, including the ark, was the shadow or pattern of the heavenly things. Therefore, the design of the Mercy Seat should be considered somewhat of a replica of God's throne. It would be appropriate to assume that there are cherubims positioned on both sides of God's throne, inasmuch as the cherubims' wings cover the Mercy Seat on the ark. This too is a pattern of heavenly realities, where cherubims' wings actually cover God's throne. This could *possibly* give us an explanation of the designation given to Satan as the *"Covering Cherub."*

The most important aspect of Ezekiel's prophecy that I would like to emphasize is Lucifer being referred as the *"Anointed"* Cherub. As we have already seen from this text, Lucifer was endowed with tremendous responsibility, beauty, wisdom, and power. However, as we look again to the 28th chapter, the prophet reveals the nature of Lucifer's fall. Beginning at verse 16, the passage says:

> By the multitude of thy merchandise they have filled the midst of thee with violence, and thou hast sinned: therefore I will cast thee as profane out of the mountain of God: and I will destroy thee, O covering cherub, from the midst of the stones of fire. Thine heart was lifted up because of thy beauty, thou hast corrupted thy wisdom by reason of thy brightness: I will cast thee to the ground, I will lay thee before kings, that they may behold thee.
>
> Ezekiel 28:16-17, KJV

In these verses we learn something very interesting about Satan. In the

KJV, verse 16 says, *"By the multitude of thy merchandise."* In the NASB it says, *"By the abundance of your trade."* The NIV renders the phrase *"through your widespread trade...."* Here we are getting a glimpse of what partly led to Satan's downfall—his abundance of *wealth and commerce* that fed into an exalted sense of pride. Here, some commentators say that this was the king of Tyre's (Ethbaal II) attribute, while others say it was Satan's. However, it really doesn't make a difference, because the principle is the same. Unrestrained passion for or the pursuit of materialism and wealth is corrupting whether it happens among humans or angels.

As this text clearly tells us, Satan was cast out of God's holy mountain as a *profane thing*. Because of his vanity, iniquity, and pride, his perfect wisdom was transformed into wicked intelligence. His supportive functionary role was transformed into opposition and antagonism. Now a rebellious cherub, Satan led a failed coup attempt and was summarily cast out of heaven. Lucifer, now defeated and frustrated, uses all of his power (his anointing) to wage war against the kingdom of God and the Church. The anointing and authority that coincided with his prestigious position in heaven are now used to steal, kill, and destroy on earth.

Although Satan is a fallen angel, he is still considered a dignitary among the angelic host. He is the God of this present world [age] (2 Cor. 4:4, John 12:31, 14:30, 1 John 5:19). In the book of Jude in verses 8 and 9, Jude speaks of the sin of speaking evil of dignitaries. To stress this point, he quotes from the Apocryphal book called *The Assumption of Moses.*[69] The text says: *"Yet Michael the archangel, when contending with the devil he disputed about the body of Moses, durst not bring against him a railing accusation, but said the Lord rebuke thee."* Though Satan was indeed the enemy of God, Satan is still in authority in the world. Therefore, I believe, that Michael the Archangel *durst* not, or *dared* not, to bring a slanderous accusation against him. Not because Satan was better, smarter, or stronger than Michael, but because down here on earth, this is Satan's kingdom—for now.

THE ANTI-CHRIST

When the Lord was in the wilderness on his forty-day fast, Satan came to him with three very pivotal temptations. Of the three, one of them particularly accentuates Satan's ultimate evil agenda. Satan offered Christ all the kingdoms of this world, along with their glory, if Jesus would bow down and worship him. Satan has always wanted to be *"like the most high."* However, his perverted lust for power and reverence will eventually be realized here on earth, through the dictatorship of the *Anti-Christ.*

In the Gospel of St. Matthew, chapter 24, verse 24, Jesus warns against false christs that shall come, by saying: *"For there shall arise false christs and false prophets, and shall shew great signs and wonders; insomuch that if it were possible, they shall deceive the very elect."* Therefore, let's turn our attention to the *Anti-Christ.* The term Anti-Christ comes from the Greek words *antee,* which means "opposite," or "instead of," and *christos,* which means *"Anointed"* and is translated *"Christ."* Together these words form the Greek word *antechristos,*[70] which translates into the "opponent of Christ," or *"instead of Christ."* In its singular form, the word *Anti-christ* is found only four times in the New Testament, and in its plural form, it's only found once. Regardless, these words are found only in the epistles of John.

In 1 John 2, the apostle states *"...and as ye have heard that the antichrist shall come, even now are there many antichrists; whereby we know that it is the last time* (1 John 2:18). Also in the 4th chapter of the same epistle, John says *"... and this is that spirit of anti-Christ, whereof ye have heard that it should come; and even now already is in the world"* (1 John 4:3). We can glean some important truths about the anti-christ from both of these passages. In this text, the *many* anti-christs alluded to are the forerunners of the apocalyptical *Beast* depicted in Revelation 13. However, there is also a *spirit* of anti-christ whose major thrust is to oppose all that pertains to the truth about Jesus Christ.

THE ANTI-ANOINTING

Comprehending the nature of the anti-christ is important to understanding the powers behind counterfeit charisma. As we examined earlier, the word *Christ* comes from the Greek word *Christos,* which means *anointed.* We also examined the word *anointed,* which comes from the Greek word, *Chrisma,* which means: *an unguent or an endowment of the Holy Spirit.* We then examined how Lucifer was an *"Anointed"* Cherub, who fell through his own pride and iniquity. When Satan fell, he didn't lose his power. His anointing was transformed for wickedness. This evil *anointing or power* is now used to oppose the kingdom of God and to wage war against it, therefore becoming an *anti-anointing* coinciding with the *anti-christ.*

In the secular world, the *anti-anointing* is manifested in a wide variety of mystical arts and occult practices such as divination, and is the power source behind *counterfeit charisma.* However, in the realm of professing Christendom, it manifests itself by mimicking the anointing and leading of the Holy Spirit. Herein is the essence of the term *"anti-anointing."* The prefix *anti-*indicates *instead of* the Holy Spirit. Since Satan transforms himself into an angel of light, he also transforms his ministers into ministers of righteousness (2 Cor. 11:13-15). The ranks of these anti-anointed ministers include false apostles, prophets, ministers, and brethren. All these can be found in local churches throughout the world. Their purpose is to deceive others while they are also being deceived. These are the *"workers of iniquity"* (Matt. 7:21-23) whom Christ *never* knew. Nothing can be more bone-chilling than to prophesy, cast out devils, or perform miracles all in Jesus' name, but on Judgment Day be condemned as one who never knew Christ.

THE EPITOME OF FALSE PROPHETS

In first John, the apostle warns of the coming of the anti-christ, based on the fact that there were already many anti-christs that had come onto the scene in John's day (1 John 2:18). I also believe this same concept certainly applies to the false prophets. The fact that we have many false prophets now anticipates the coming of the greatest false prophet of them all. In Revelation 13, we read about the false prophet of the Apocalypse:

> He performs great signs (startling miracles), even making fire fall from the sky to the earth in men's sight. And because of the signs (miracles) which he is allowed to perform in the presence of the [first] beast, he deceives those who inhabit the earth, commanding them to erect a statue (an image) in the likeness of the beast who was wounded by the [small] sword and still lived. And he is permitted [also] to impart the breath of life into the beast's image, so that the statue of the beast could actually talk and cause to be put to death those who would not bow down *and* worship the image of the beast.
>
> Revelation 13:13-15, AMP

Time does not permit a thorough examination of this text; however, a few aspects need to be examined. First of all, the false prophet will be able to perform astonishing miracles, some reminiscent of God sending down fire from heaven (Gen. 19:14, 1 Kings 18:38, 1 Chron. 21:26), but even greater than that, "And he is permitted [also] to impart the breath of life into the beast's image, so that the statue of the beast could actually talk and cause to be put to death those who would not bow down *and* worship the image of the beast." Imagine that, an inanimate statue being brought to life! This appears to be a miracle on the same order of *Jannes and Jambres'* wooden rods being turned to living snakes—miraculous but wicked. This is why you cannot be caught up in seeking signs and wonders: not all supernatural occurrences and miraculous events come from God. The spiritually immature are drawn to such displays, because they do not have their senses exercised to discern good from evil. Jesus warned, "an adulterous generation seeks after signs" (Matt.12:39).

Finally, there are many false prophets outside of the Church and

Christendom in general, those who are spiritists, mediums, psychics, soothsayers, fortunetellers, and the like. All these are a given. However, our focus has been on those who operate in the churches using counterfeit gifts in Jesus' name. These are the ones that the Lord specifically condemns in Matthew 7:21-23, who will claim, "Lord, Lord…!" In Acts 13:6, we find an example of a false prophet that was connected to the demonic. The text reads, "now when they had gone through the island to Paphos, they found a certain sorcerer, a false prophet, a Jew whose name *was* Bar-Jesus" (NKJV). Here we have one named *Bar-Jesus* who was a *sorcerer* and a *false prophet*. Imagine that, a false prophet engaged in sorcery. Remember, the definition of sorcery is *the use of supernatural power over others through the assistance of spirits….*" False prophets do not go around calling themselves false prophets. Since they are deceived, they think they are real prophets, and they believe the voice they hear is God's voice. But *Bar-Jesus* is a type of false prophet with power, because they are connected to demons who give them supernatural abilities through sorcery, and impart doctrines of devils or demons through them. For this very reason, you must be careful whom it is that you follow.

Another end-time prophecy concerning those who follow false prophets is found in 2 Thessalonians 2, where the apostle Paul warns:

> The coming of the *lawless one* is according to the working of Satan, with all power, signs, and lying wonders, and with all unrighteous deception among those who perish, because they did not receive the love of the truth, that they might be saved. And for this reason God will send them strong delusion, that they should believe the lie, that they all may be condemned who did not believe the truth but had pleasure in unrighteousness.
> 2 Thessalonians 2:9-12, NKJV

This passage is powerful. During the time of the anti-christ (the lawless one), the Scripture clearly identifies Satan's array of power in the form of signs and lying wonders with all deception among those who perish. In the previous chapters we have identified those who follow false prophets as being the type who will not endure sound doctrine, have itching ears, ever learning but never coming to the knowledge of the truth. They would rather hear lies and niceties from their prophets, instead of hearing the truth that brings conviction and repentance. In 2 Thes. 2:9-12, the same group is identified. Of these the apostle declares, "because they did not receive the love of the truth, that they might be saved." This is very concerning, because as we have learned in this book, false prophets work in congregations that create the environment to facilitate false prophecy going forth; they are only comfortable and welcomed in certain congregations.

Since these congregations have rejected truth and prefer a lie, God turns them over to strong delusion so that they will believe a lie. If God turns someone, there is absolutely no hope for that individual. If Satan is your enemy, God is your help. But if God is your enemy, there is no help for you. Within His own providence and purpose, God determines who and when He will turn people over to a reprobate mind (Rom. 1:28). God determines whose heart He will harden (Rom. 9:18). It was God who determined that He would send a lying spirit to be in the mouths of Ahab's false prophets (1 Kings 22:19-23). When God sends strong delusion, there is no coming back from that. Even though they might hear the truth, they will believe the lie just like Ahab.

Thus says the LORD of hosts: Do not listen to the words of the [false] prophets who prophesy to you. They teach you vanity (emptiness, falsity, and futility) and fill you with vain hopes; they speak a vision of their own minds and not from the mouth of the LORD.

Jeremiah 23:16, AMP

CHAPTER 9

THE SPIRIT OF THIS WORLD

In the first epistle of John, we find a powerful passage of Scripture that encapsulates the spirit of this present world. The passage reads,

> Love not the world, neither the things *that are* in the world. If any man love the world, the love of the Father is not in him. For all that *is* in the world, the lust of the flesh, and the lust of the eyes, and the pride of life, is not of the Father, but is of the world. And the world passeth away, and the lust thereof: but he that doeth the will of God abideth for ever.
>
> 1 John 2:15-17, KJV

In this passage, we have a clear warning about the world (this current world system), which is set up after the dictates of Satan, who is *the god of this world* and *the prince and the power of the air* (2 Cor. 4:4, Eph. 2:2). Everything in the world has in some way or another been tainted by satanic influence. The local churches are not immune to this. It's simply the way the world is, and how it operates. It is interesting that here the apostle emphasizes two mutually exclusive things. In verse 15, he warns, "If any man love the world, the love of the Father is not in him…" This is a hard saying, but it is true. You cannot have the love of God and the love of the world system dwell in you simultaneously. This is because the world system is under the control of Satan. John

> *Pride and lustful ambition for wealth and power are not fruits of the Spirit, but stem from covetousness and the deception of selfish ambition, which are works of the flesh, not the Spirit.*

also writes, "…and that the whole world is under the control of the evil one" (1 John 5:19). Therefore, if you love the world, you are loving Satan's world and what he has to offer which excludes the love of the Father from being in you.

Let's determine what is meant by loving the world. Does it mean that as Christians we cannot enjoy the fruit of our labor through things in the world that God has created for our enjoyment? Does it mean that if we work hard we cannot have a decent home in which to live, and be able to provide for our families? Of course not. What is meant here is not so much the *materials* in the world as the *materialism* that drives inordinate ambitions to obtain material things. As James Montgomery Boice asserts, "A person without worldly goods can be just as materialistic as a person who has many of them."[71] So it is not so much the things as it is the attitude about achieving these things that is dominant in a satanically controlled world system. There are those who will do anything to get ahead: lie, steal, kill, or compromise, anything to obtain their perception of success.

The reason why the love for this world is mutually exclusive from the love of the father is because of what the apostle describes in verse 16: "For all that *is* in the world, the lust of the flesh, and the lust of the eyes, and the pride of life, is not of the Father, but is of the world." By these three are men snared, to drown in perdition. What we see, we want. We pursue things to experience pleasure and gratification of lustful passions to satisfy the flesh, and we define ourselves by the status we achieve based upon the approval, dictates, and standards this world sets. Therefore, through the love of the world, Satan entices through the eyes, the flesh, and through pride.

We see these three operating is in the *Garden of Eden* when the serpent tempted Eve (Gen. 3:1-6). Satan through the serpent said, eat and *you will be like God*, (the pride of life, appealing to her ambition) when she *saw* that the fruit was good and desirable (making the visual connection to the forbidden fruit, enticing her desire through the gateway of the eyes) and she saw that the fruit was "good for food" (satisfying the desire and craving to consume and eat to appease the appetite—the lust of the flesh). It was through these three that brought the fall of the first Adam.

We find these three again with Jesus Christ the second Adam was tempted in the wilderness by the Devil. "The devil said to him, 'If you are the Son of God, tell this stone to become bread'" (Luke 4:3). Jesus fasted for forty days, and naturally he was hungry. This attack targeted the lust of the flesh, part of which is the base desire to consume and eat. Skipping to the third temptation, the Devil led him to Jerusalem and had him stand on the highest point of the temple. "If you are the Son of God," he said, "throw yourself down from here. For it is written: 'He will command his angels concerning you to guard you carefully; they will lift you up in their hands, so that you will not strike your foot against a stone'" (Luke 4:9-11). By asserting that since you are God's son, you are a deity, too important and precious for anything disastrous to happen to you, God will make an exception for you. This temptation targets pride.

Finally, the temptation that is most important to this aspect of our study is the second one. "The devil led him up to a high place and *showed him* in an instant all the kingdoms of the world. And he said to him, 'I will give you all their authority and splendor; it has been given to me, and I can give it to anyone I want to. If you worship me, it will all be yours'" (Luke 4:5-7). This is truly another miraculous event. Satan showed Jesus all the world's kingdoms along with their splendor and glory. That alone takes power, but here he is appealing to Jesus through the lust of the eye, because he "showed" Jesus these kingdoms and then offered them to Him. The devil affirmed the fact that they were his to give. The kingdoms of this world are what Satan will eventually give to the anti-christ.

However, the point is that the wealth and riches of this world's system are under the direct control of Satan, and he uses the lust of the flesh, the lust of the eye, and the pride of life to draw people into loving this world system, and thereby serving him. John states, "If any man love the world, the love of the Father is not in him," because these are mutually exclusive. This is why there are so many warnings in the Bible to those who want to become rich and famous in this world (see chapter 5), because people who love material things and materialism invariably also love the world. It doesn't matter if you profess to be a Christian, attend a church, or are in the ministry. Pride and lustful ambition for wealth and power are not fruits of the Spirit, but stem from covetousness and the deception of selfish ambition (see Gal. 5:20, emulations KJV, canvassing for position),[72] which are works of the flesh, not the Spirit.

Back to False Prophets

All of this is important to our study, because false prophets are not connected to God, nor are they hearing from heaven. However, when a false prophet claims that they receive "a word" or a message supernaturally, they may be telling the truth! They *are* hearing from "a spirit," but not the Holy Spirit. They are hearing from a deceiving, lying spirit. Satan does not care if you attribute things to God that are really from him. Satan is a liar and a deceiver. Since a "word from God" is not an option for them, their prophecies are restricted to things pertaining to this world. Throughout the Bible narrative, Satan's messengers have always been limited in what signs and wonders they could perform, because Satan is limited.

> *False prophets encourage people to seek the things that foster covetousness for materialism, wealth, prosperity, cessation of adversity, and ease of life. Through their so-called deep, prophetic messages, these deceivers are really messengers of seduction enticing people to move away from God to the world.*

In this corrupt world system, it is Satan that offers the kingdoms of this world and all their glory, riches, splendor, fame, power, success, connections, and influence. The reason why false prophets typically prophesy about money, wealth, materialism, fame, and influence is because these are all the things that pertain to the world system. They speak of the world, because they have no access to God or heaven. They cannot give you an authentic word from God, because a false prophet does not hear God's voice. They hear the voice of the world and do mind the things pertaining to this world. For this reason, their so-called prophecies can only give insignificant information that have no deliverance in them, superfluous details such as a phone number, a name, an address, or what simply amounts to fortunetelling. Prophesying about getting a car, a house, job, or that some money is coming your way is all they can prophesy. All these things pertain to the world and cause you to desire the things of the world through lust.

In James, the apostle admonishes:

> When you ask, you do not receive, because you ask with wrong motives, that you may spend what you get on your pleasures. You adulterous people, don't you know that friendship with the world means enmity against God? Therefore, anyone who chooses to be a friend of the world becomes an enemy of God.
>
> James 4:3-4

People want to serve God on their terms. The deceived really do not want God in their lives. They're not interested in living a holy and acceptable life for God. What they really want is what amounts to a celestial Santa Claus, who will bless them with goodies whenever they ask for it. They want a heavenly janitor who will clean up their life's messes, instead of them being obedient and living righteously in the first place. They are not interested in a loving relationship with the Lord; they just want a God that will satisfy their greed and lusts. This is why James addresses this folly in rather direct terms, because a relationship with God is serious. God is not playing games. The Lord declares, "I know your motives," and He will not appease a lustful, covetous person by giving them whatever just because they ask for it.

God sees covetous people as being spiritually *adulterous*, because they are trying to have a relationship with Him and the world. They are trying to have two lovers. But God draws a clear line of demarcation when He says, "Therefore, anyone who chooses to be a friend of the world becomes an enemy of God." It is important to point out how asking with wrong motives is correlated directly to loving the world. The reason is, in order to want those things of the world, you have to be enticed by what the world has to offer. This is why Satan tempted Jesus by showing him the kingdoms of this world and all their splendor and glory.

False prophets encourage people to seek the things that foster covetousness for materialism, wealth, prosperity, cessation of adversity, and ease of life. Through their so-called deep, prophetic messages, these deceivers are really messengers of seduction enticing people to move away from God to the world, no matter how often they invoke God's name or quote the Scriptures in the process. So what that they are eloquent and know the Bible? Satan quoted Scripture to tempt Jesus (Psalms 91:11-12 with Luke 4:9-11). And James also says that, "the devils believe" (James 2:19).

THE ANGEL WITH A CHECK

The following is an example of how easy it is to lead someone astray by enticing people with the things of this world. I recently saw a false prophet on the internet that began prophesying to a young man during a church service. Before he started prophesying, he began scanning the audience as if he were searching for the right person. Then he called out this man from the audience who just so happened to be sitting in the front row. To him the false prophet said, "Come." Then he began prophesying, saying, "I saw an angel standing next to you, and angel was holding a check." After hearing this, the man from the audience fell to his knees. Then the false prophet said, "The angel then stood in front of you and said to you, whatever has gone on financially... it started in 2016." Then the prophet said, "The Lord opened my eyes and I saw you selling, and you were building apartment complexes." Then he said, "I'm a prophet." After he said that, the people started clapping, but he told them: "Wait."

He then started prophesying again: "In the angel's hand was a check... and the check was for 1.29 million dollars, and I saw a name on the check." Then he started spelling the man's first name, calling out the letters of his first name slowly. Then he whispered the man's name. The man said, "That's my name." All the people started clapping again, but this time the prophet received the applause. Once again, this is the type of folly that is played out all over the world. An angel with a check? Who could believe something so ridiculous? Sadly to say, too many people.

Considering what we have covered in 1 John 2:15-17, what do we see in this prophetic exchange? Who is being glorified—God or things that appeal to the lust of the flesh, the lust of the eye, or the pride of life? Does such a prophecy honor God, or does it support the things pertaining to the spirit of this world? The prophet said that the Lord opened his eyes and saw the man selling, and the man was going to build apartment complexes. That's commerce. That's urban development. That's money in the bank. None of these things get you closer to God, because the Bible says, "what good does it do if a man gain the whole world and loose his soul" (Matt. 6:26)? The Bible says of Satan, "through the multitude of thy merchandise they have filled thee with violence and thou hast sinned" (Ezek. 28:16, KJV). All these things promote loving this world. It's the same spirit that Nebuchadnezzar had when he said, "is this not Babylon the great city that I have built" (Dan. 4:30)? Where in Scripture has one of God's holy angels ever brought a human being some money, let alone a check? As ridiculous as this was, the people in that church still applauded as though they had witnessed some great prophetic work.

In 1 Corinthians, here is what the apostle Paul says about prophecy,

> But if an unbeliever or an inquirer comes in while everyone is prophesying, they are convicted of sin and are brought under judgment by all, as the secrets of their hearts are laid bare. So they will fall down and worship God, exclaiming, "God is really among you!"
>
> 1 Corinthians 14:24-25

Notice the focus of prophecy in this passage. It has nothing to do with receiving fame, fortune, or wealth. It has nothing to do with glorifying anyone's flesh. Paul could have used any number of hypothetical circumstances to give an example of the purpose and effectiveness of prophecy, but he chose a scenario that addresses a *sinner* or *inquirer* coming into a church where "true" prophecy is going forth and the effect it would have on such a person. "…they are convicted of sin and are brought under judgment by all, as the secrets of their hearts are laid bare. So they will fall down and worship God, exclaiming, "God is really among you!" This is what real prophecy does: convicts of sin, brings deliverance, and glorifies God, but *never* encourages the love of things of this world. A false prophet encourages people to love the things of this world by prophesying that God is going to give them things to consume upon their lust. As a matter of fact, He promises that he won't give you anything under those conditions (James 4:3-4).

In Genesis 14:23, Abram (Abraham) refused to receive the deceitfulness of riches when he declined taking anything from the king of Sodom after winning the battle against the kings. Abram stated, "...I will not *take* from a thread even to a shoe latchet, and that I will not take any thing that *is* thine, lest thou shouldest say, I have made Abram rich" (KJV). Abram understood that by taking anything from Sodom, he would not be able to say his dependence and source was God, from whom all good and perfect gifts flow. Abram refused to let the king of Sodom (the world) have the bragging rights. Taking the spoils of war from the king would have impugned his spiritual standing. Therefore, Abram rightfully rejected the offer.[73]

Like Abraham, we must discern the spirit of what is being said. We must ask, is this bringing us closer to God, or to the world? So if someone prophesies about getting a car, money, or things pertaining to this world, even if it comes true, that's promoting loving the things of this world, because your affections become directed towards receiving the things. Remember, "seek ye first the kingdom of God, and his righteousness and the things will be added." No one can bless you better than God, and you don't need a prophet to tell you that there is an angel with a check with your name on it!

THE INQUIRER IS JUST AS GUILTY AS THE FALSE PROPHET

In chapter 3, we covered how it is the people that create the environment for a false prophet to thrive. What we learned was that people who do not want to hear the truth, conform to sound doctrine, or have a close relationship with the Lord are the ones who are not truly interested in growing in grace, but are only interested in what's in it for them. These are the type that are ever learning but never coming to the knowledge of the truth. They have a form of godliness, but they deny the power that could bring conviction and deliverance into their lives. Of these, the Scriptures declare that they have itching ears who will seek out teachers and false prophets, who reject sound doctrine but prefer fables and lies (2 Tim. 4:3). Jeremiah gives this pointed rebuke when he declares,

> For this is a rebellious people, faithless *and* lying sons, children who will not hear the law *and* instruction of the Lord; Who [virtually] say to the seers [by their conduct], See not! and to the prophets, Prophesy not to us what is right! Speak to us smooth things, prophesy deceitful illusions.
>
> Isaiah 30:9-10, AMP

Deceitful illusions like an angel holding a million-dollar check! First of all, false prophets only swim in certain ponds. You will not find them in any churches that are committed to teaching sound doctrine. You will only find them in churches that put emphasis on seeking signs and wonders. These prophetic liars are perfectly suited for churches that claim that the Spirit moves and has His way, which often equates to a church that lacks structure and order, and has no checks or balances to guard against false doctrine. These churches are typically very emotional but lacking substance or depth. In churches like this, people equate experience with a relationship with God. By being experience-oriented and seekers of signs and wonders, they are ripe for the picking for a false prophet or counterfeit minister. However, the recipient and those who seek the false prophet are not innocent in this transaction. This is what the prophet Ezekiel has to say:

> [The prophet has not been granted permission to give an answer to the hypocritical inquirer] but if the prophet does give the man the answer he desires [thus allowing himself to be a party to the inquirer's sin], I the Lord will see to it that the prophet is deceived in his answer, and I will stretch out My hand against him and will destroy him from the midst of My people Israel.

And they both shall bear the punishment of their iniquity: the iniquity of the [presumptuous] prophet shall
be the same as the iniquity of the [hypocritical] inquirer.
Ezekiel 14:9-10, AMP

This passage is a clear warning. Those who consult with a false prophet are just as guilty as the false prophet. God is not giving passes for
those who follow the lead of a deceiver. The Lord has warned that in
the last days many false prophets shall arise and shall deceive many.
This brings to mind the nine hundred and nine lost souls that were
murdered and committed mass suicide in one of the worst examples
of what can happen when people follow a false prophet. Right before
Jim Jones—who started out calling himself a pastor, then a prophet, and then even God—ordered the people to drink cyanide-laced
Kool-Aid, to justify the suicide this is what he quoted, "No man taketh
my life from me, but I lay it down." In the background, you hear the
people shouting and their applause.[74] This deranged man had the audacity to quote Jesus' words, to justify commanding nine hundred and
nine people to kill themselves.

As tragic as this was, both the prophet and the people perished in the
jungles of Guyana without hope. When their bodies were transported
back to the United States, over four-hundred bodies were unclaimed
and therefore buried in a mass grave. What a sad epitaph for those
poor souls who decided to follow a deceiving false prophet. The Bible
declares that it is wicked to inquire of a false prophet. Why? Because
a false prophet could actually be practicing any form of divination, be
demon-influenced, and even demon-possessed. Therefore, the iniquity
of the [presumptuous] prophet shall be the same as the iniquity of the
[hypocritical] inquirer, because they both drink the bitter waters that
flow from the same corrupt fountain.

Let's peel back another layer dealing with the destructive impact of
false prophets. In 2 Peter 2:1-2, the passage reads:

> But there were also false prophets among the people, just as there will be false teachers among you. They will secretly introduce destructive heresies, even denying the sovereign Lord who bought them—bringing swift destruction on themselves. Many will follow their depraved conduct and will bring the way of truth into disrepute.
>
> 2 Peter 2:1-2

In this passage, we are given a solemn warning concerning the destruction that false prophets and teachers can bring to a congregation. The apostle says that they shall "secretly bring in destructive heresies." Since they stand before the congregation, the false prophets are hardly teaching in secret. Here, *secretly bringing in* should be understood as "to cause something to happen by introducing factors from outside."[75] *Outside* meaning outside of the congregation or outside of the whole counsel of God taught in the Scriptures. Peter categorizes these teachings as *destructive*, not in a temporal or material sense, but meaning that they will "send them to hell."[76] Therefore, understanding the problem with the teachings or so-called revelations from false prophets is no trivial matter, but can have a devastating effect on the receiver's eternal destiny. This is not a cavalier exercise without consequences. People are being misled and facing damnation. Unfortunately, how quick we are to excuse the antics of the false prophets of today as just one of many acceptable practices in the churches.

It is important that the author reiterate that Joel's prophecy in Acts 2:17 anticipates a prophetic movement where young men and women, handmaidens, and servants will prophesy, see visions, and have dreams. Clearly, the fulfillment of this has been ongoing since the day of Pentecost. Again, true prophets are not the main focus of this book, but the advent of the many false prophets that shall be characteristic of the signs of the end-times given by the Lord during his Mount Olivet discourse.

THE SCHOOLS OF THE PROPHETS

Many of the people who claim to be prophets are products of the "schools of prophets" popping up all over the country, and seems to at least to some degree, a move to legitimize *this particular* neo-prophetic movement. In America, anyone can start a religious school. As long as they are not issuing "a degree," in most states it's probably not illegal. Some of those who advocate for the schools of prophets do so on biblical and extra-biblical grounds. One of the extra-biblical sources is the *Easton Bible Dictionary* article concerning the *schools of prophets*, which basically states that "schools of the prophets" were developed specifically for training prophets. The Scriptural references Easton uses for this concept are found in(1Sa 19:18-24; 2Ki 2:3, 15; 2Ki 4:38). These "schools" were established at Ramah, Bethel, Gilgal, Gibeah, and Jericho.[77]

However, an opposing view against the schools of prophets is based upon the observation that a mistranslation of the texts is found in 2 Kings 22:14 and 2 Chron. 34:22, where the word *mishneh*[78] is translated *college* by the *King James* translators. The word is usually translated "second or double" and is never translated as *college* in any other use in the Bible.[79] Therefore, according to 2 Kings 22:14 and 2 Chron. 34:22, the word should be rendered *the Second District* or *"mishneh quarter"* of Jerusalem, which was a "second" New Quarter (see Zeph. 1:10, Neh. 3:9, 12) built to the northwest of the original Jerusalem. The "college" translation was based on a *later* secondary meaning of the Hebrew word *mishneh*.[80]

There are certainly no Scriptural references that indicate that any of the Old Testament prophets of God, like Moses, Isaiah, Jeremiah, and others, ever attended a school to perfect the trade of being a prophet. As for those "groups of prophets" that are referred to in Scriptures, not a lot is known about the origin of such groups. Obviously the groups of pagan prophets, i.e., prophets of Baal, qualify as false prophets. There is no Biblical evidence that God called a group of prophets simultaneously. Prophets were called as individuals.[81]

Whatever side of the debate you fall on, the fact is today there are many *schools of prophets*. On one hand this could be seen as a positive, because hopefully these schools give some training that could improve one's ministry and Christian walk and life of service. However, and most importantly, there is the negative side, which would be if the students, once completing their prophetic school's curriculum, were ordained during a service where the title prophet would be conferred upon them. This is a frightening proposition when you consider an individual believing themselves to be a prophet based on the word "prophet" being written on a certificate of ordination. If they are being made prophets by men, then they are not prophets called by God. However, since we cannot confirm what God has spoken to someone's heart as to how and when someone is called, we must then discern the message as well as the life of the messenger. Even from the Old Testament, this has always been the way to tell the difference, because callings are subjective experiences.

In the New Testament, speaking specifically of false prophets, Jesus declared, "you will know them by their fruits" (Matt. 7:15-20). And as to the last days, the Bible is very clear: many false prophets shall arise and deceive many (Matt 25:11, 1 John 4:1). Jesus warned, "see to it that no man deceives you." Those who claim to be a "good" prophet because they are eighty percent accurate fail to understand that also means that twenty percent of the time, they give false prophecies. Finally, accuracy is not the only criterion to distinguish between a true and false prophet. It is the source of the message from which the prophet speaks that determines whether it is of God or not.

CHAPTER 10

ORDER IN THE CHURCH

Throughout the narrative of this book, we have covered many aspects of prophecy. After all is said and done, the question remains: What does the Bible have to say about the purpose and practice of prophecy in the church? On one end of the spectrum, there are many that hold to the position that there are no prophets or the gift of prophecy in the church today. On the other end, some hold that anyone declaring the Word of God by forth-telling (preaching) is prophesying. Then in the middle are those who don't know, don't care, or do not have an opinion either way. Yet, amongst all the speculation and debate, in certain quarters of Christianity a prophetic movement is spreading like wildfire across America and in many parts of the world. The question is, does this surge of "prophets" actually support the fulfillment of Biblical prophecy that many false prophets shall rise in these last days?

Based upon the writings in the New Testament epistles, prophets and prophecy in the Church cannot be denied. Even though there are many that teach that there are no prophets today, on that point we will have to agree to disagree. However, though I may disagree with the "there are no prophets today" position, I do so with great pause. I must acknowledge that there is a very slippery slope concerning individuals receiving subjective revelation, because of the potential to spread false doctrine and false prophecies that can cause harm to others. I believe that there is prophecy today, but not because there are ministers around today that call themselves prophets. No, I believe there is prophecy because the Bible declares that prophets are in the

Church. Therefore, I am not willing to go as far as many conservative and evangelical commentators and scholars do when they interpret "prophecies shall cease" (1 Cor. 13:8) to mean that when the canon of Scriptures was closed, prophecy ended. Though they hold tight to that conclusion, it is not a conclusion that is explicitly stated in the Scriptures.

It is interesting that Scriptures warn us to test the spirits to see if they are of God, because many false prophets have gone out into the world. However, Scriptures do not say, "Reject all prophecy because there are no more prophets." No, according to apostolic writing, prophecy has been understood to be a gift that would continue through the Church age, because the testimony of Jesus Christ is the spirit of prophecy (Rev. 19:10). Therefore, as long as the testimony of Jesus is still active, no one can preclude prophecy. However, Acts gives us some information about prophecy that would characterize the entire Church age:

> And it shall come to pass in the last days, saith God, I will pour out of my Spirit upon all flesh: and your sons and your daughters shall prophesy, and your young men shall see visions, and your old men shall dream dreams: And on my servants and on my handmaidens I will pour out in those days of my Spirit; and they shall prophesy:
>
> Acts 2:17-18, KJV

In this passage, Dr. Luke records Peter's powerful sermon on the Day of Pentecost, which includes a quote from Joel's prophecy (Joel 2:28-32), where it says, "...in the last days I will pour out of my Spirit upon all flesh: and your sons and your daughters shall prophesy." In reference to the *pouring out of the Spirit*, the phrase "in the last days" cannot be overlooked. Since the Spirit was poured out on the Day of Pentecost, in a broader sense we have been in the *last days* since that time. However, the term "last days" can also be equated with the "end times," which means the *last days* right before the coming of the Lord. In either case, whether one applies a broader or narrower view to this phrase, it doesn't change the fact that the outpouring of the Spirit would enable the gift of prophecy throughout the era followed by the outpouring. Therefore, to say that prophecy has stopped pushes human reasoning above God's purpose and providence. No matter what position one holds on the use and function and viability of prophecy, the fact is, Scripture declares that during the last days, the prophetic phenomenon would be present. How the actual function and fulfillment of that prophecy plays out is open for debate.

Though I understand the reason why there are those who disagree, the Bible does address the contention against prophecy. For example, in 1 Thessalonians 5:19-21, Paul gives us this instruction: "Quench not the Spirit. Despise not prophesyings. Prove all things; hold fast that which is good" (KJV). In this passage, the apostle is making a point that refusing to let the gift of prophecy flow is tantamount to quenching the Spirit. Evidentially, in Paul's day, even as it is still to this day, people were getting carried away with the use of spiritual gifts, and false prophecy was a problem. However, the fact that the gifts needed to be managed does not negate their reality or significance. The *Pillar Commentary* says it this way: "*Do not put out the Spirit's fire; do not treat prophecies with contempt.*"[82]

In 2 Thessalonians, there was an incident where this congregation received a false teaching concerning the Day of the Lord, which had a drastic effect among some of the congregates. Paul directly addresses this issue in 2 Thes. 2:2. Apparently there was a bogus letter, claiming to be from an apostle, stating that the Day of the Lord had already come. But the fact that there are frauds actually supports the fact that the real McCoys exist. No one counterfeits something that is not real.

Speaking of 1 Thessalonians 5:19-21, *Kenneth Wuest's Expanded Translation* says it this way: "Stop stifling and suppressing the Spirit. Stop counting as nothing divine revelations given in the local assembly by the one who receives them, but putting all things to the test for the purpose of approving them…"[83] From this passage we can conclude that it would be an overreaction to forbid the Spirit to speak through prophecy to a congregation. The response to that mindset is to "stop stifling or quenching the Spirit," but rather to "test or prove all things holding on to that which is good." F.F. Bruce states, that this reference may primarily be to prophetic utterances, recognized as being divinely inspired and should receive careful attention and be translated into appropriate action.[84]

As I stated in the Introduction, the focus of Old Testament prophecy has been revealed in Christ. The New Testament focus of prophecy has changed to what Christ has to say primarily to the Church and about the coming of His kingdom in full manifestation, which anticipates His second coming, the culminating prophetic event of this age. Christ's message to the Church is therefore the central focus and foundation of prophetic revelation in the New Testament. As declared in the book of Revelation, "the testimony of Jesus, is the spirit of prophecy" (Rev. 19:10). It is this same "testimony of Jesus" that is to be the driving force behind the *spirit of prophecy* which comes to build Christ's Church through edification, exhortation, and comfort in the Church (1 Cor. 14:3). Prophecy in the Church was never meant to be a platform to entice people about materialism or about the acquiring of the riches of this world. The very reason the Church of Laodicea was rebuked was because they were steeped in materialism. The Lord said, "So then because thou art lukewarm, and neither cold nor hot, I will spue thee out of my mouth. Because thou sayest, I am rich, and increased with goods, and have need of nothing; and knowest not that thou art wretched, and miserable, and poor, and blind, and naked…" (Rev.3:16-17, KJV).

In Ephesians 4, we are informed about the purpose for the five-fold ministry gifts (apostles, prophets, evangelists, pastors, and teachers):

And he gave the apostles, the prophets, the evangelists, the shepherds and teachers, to equip the saints for the work of ministry, for building up the body of Christ, until we all attain to the unity of the faith and of the knowledge of the Son of God, to mature manhood, to the measure of the stature of the fullness of Christ, so that we may no longer be children, tossed to and fro by the waves and carried about by every wind of doctrine, by human cunning, by craftiness in deceitful schemes.

Ephesians 4:11-14, ESV

You don't need a doctorate in theology or an advanced degree in ancient Greek to understand this passage, because it speaks plainly. The passage begins with "He Himself gave some...." These four words are clear. Christ Himself is the one who gives these gifts to the Church. The fact that He gives only "some" is in direct opposition to the "many" false prophets who historically have always outnumbered true prophets. It was Jesus that declared, "I will build my church..." (Matt. 16:18). Unambiguously, Christ is saying that He personally is the one who chooses specific ministry gifts to use in His enterprise to build His Church. Since it is His Church, He alone decides what the purpose for the ministry gifts will be.

THE FIRST PURPOSE

The first purpose for the ministry gifts, in this case prophets, was *"for the equipping of the saints for the work of ministry."* Now, this passage is not saying that all saints should be trained as pulpit ministers, but for service, i.e., the ministry of helps, hospitality, giving, etc., service that will help strengthen the functioning of the church through equipping, preparing, training, and discipling.

THE SECOND PURPOSE

For the edifying of the body of Christ. Here the word edifying is *oikodomē,*[85] which means architecture, to build, or a building, and is akin to the word *edifice.* In this case the prophet and prophecy are to help build up the body of Christ through using their gift of keen insight and understanding of the Word of God, and utilizing their spiritual discernment to guard against the teaching and heresies of false prophets. Paul also says, "though I have *the gift of* prophecy, and understand all mysteries, and all knowledge…" (1 Cor.13:2, KJV). Their gift in the knowledge of the whole counsel of the Word of God was to be a front line in defense against false doctrine. This is also why in the Church, prophets were to be judged by other prophets. Again, Paul instructs, "Let the prophets speak two or three, and let the other judge" (1 Cor.14:29, KJV). The Body of Christ cannot be built up if you allow the teachings of false prophets that bring in damnable heresies to take root in a church.

THE THIRD PURPOSE

Till we all come to the unity of the faith and of the knowledge of the Son of God. Coming to the unity of the faith suggests that doctrinally the church is not unified in the *knowledge of the Son of God,* because many have not mastered the first principles or basics concerning righteousness and holiness, and what it means to be a Christian in a wicked world. This is a big problem that manifests itself in local churches all over the world. Therefore, the ministry gifts were to be the tools that the Lord uses to bring believers into conformity with the will of God through the Word of God, as opposed to being conformed to the present world system. The writer of Hebrews states:

> In fact, though by this time you ought to be teachers, you need someone to teach you the elementary truths of God's word all over again. You need milk, not solid food! Anyone who lives on milk, being still an infant,

is not acquainted with the teaching about righteousness. But solid food is for the mature, who by constant use
have trained themselves to distinguish good from evil.

Hebrews 5:12-14

Babes in Christ do not have their senses exercised through the constant use and having trained themselves through life's experience in
walking with the Lord. Without that, they do not have the ability to
distinguish between good and evil. This is why bringing saints in the
unity of the faith and increasing knowledge in the Son of God are critically important. True prophecy aids in this process by the utilization
of that gift through prophetic discernment and knowledge in God's
word to be a cohesive agent in the unifying process.

THE FOURTH PURPOSE

*That we should no longer be children, tossed to and fro and carried about with every
wind of doctrine.* Immature Christians are called "children," because
like children they are easily distracted with all of the foolish fanfare
of flamboyant false prophets and false doctrine. Children are not interested in a solid, healthy diet. They want fast food and instant gratification, without the understanding that what tastes good may not be
good for them. As long as carnal Christians can get their itching ears
filled with junk, they will reject a full plate of sound doctrine. Therefore, they are open for any fad doctrine that will entertain them, while
keeping them unhealthy, foolish, immature, and never coming to the
knowledge of the truth. These are those who pass up the narrow road
that leads to life, and prefer the ease and comfort on the broad road
that leads to destruction.

On the other hand, it is the five-fold ministry gifts that Jesus chose and
placed in the body to specifically address this issue and to prevent the
spiritually immature Christians from being enticed away from a sure
foundation based upon a more sure word of prophecy (2 Peter 1:16-
20). There are many doctrines blowing around these days. Much of
this foolishness is propagated by false prophets who are only out to

make merchandise out of the saints. As wolves in sheep's clothing, they feed upon the sheep. These are those the passage identifies as "the trickery of men, in the cunning craftiness of deceitful plotting…" (Eph. 4:14, NASB).

In the previous chapters of this book, I have exposed some of "the trickery of men" who plot and deceive. Anyone that the Lord did not place in the body as part of the five-fold ministry gifts—remember he only placed "some"—are false! Therefore, the true purpose of New Testament prophecy was for the purposes that the Lord has outlined in Eph.4:11-14, and in 1 Cor. 13 and 14.

Understanding that the examples of false prophecy cited in this book are anecdotal, I would like to pose the following questions: How does a prophet that claims he saw an angel with a check for 1.29 million dollars in his hand prepare someone for the work of the ministry? How does a prophet calling out someone's name, phone number, or address build up the Body of Christ? How does a prophet that uses divination to raise big offerings and fleece God's people for filthy lucre's sake bring people to the unity of the faith? How does a prophet whose prophecies about a person becoming a millionaire bring a person a perfecting to the knowledge of Christ Jesus? How does a prophet that sends out prophecies over the internet that preys on gullible, weak-minded individuals for money discourage being tossed to and fro with every wind of doctrine? The answers are obvious—they don't.

Here is what the Scriptures say about permitting the function of spiritual gifts in the church:

> What then shall we say, brothers and sisters? When you come together, each of you has a hymn, or a word of instruction, a revelation, a tongue or an interpretation. Everything must be done so that the church may be built up.
>
> 1 Corinthians 14:26

THE AGE OF FALSE PROPHETS

That last line is important, "everything must be done so that the Church is built up," not the individual exercising the gift being built up. Remember, Jesus said, "you will know false prophets by their fruits." Though a false prophet may read from a Bible and use Jesus' name, in the end it will still always be about them. This is the reason why prophecy has to be judged. Paul says, "And let two or three prophets speak, and let the others pass judgment"(1 Cor.14:29, NASB).

The word translated as *judged* or *judgment* is the Greek word *diakrinō*,[86] which means to *separate thoroughly, to discriminate, to decide.* Though the apostle is allowing for the function of spiritual gifts in the Church, it is done with the understanding that the chance for false prophecy and false doctrine exists. Therefore, other prophets, who presumably would be well versed in God's Word, would be the *discriminating* factor who could *separate thoroughly* what was being given to the Church in the form of a revelation or prophecy.

Since prophecy is something that is subject to being judged, that would indicate that the prophecy itself must be something that *can be* judged. There is no way to judge something on the spot that is to occur a year later. For this reason, it is doubtful that futuristic prophecy is what the apostle had in mind here. These prophetic utterances that are subject to being judged are those that deal with instruction and illuminations of God's Word through the ministry of the Holy Spirit. Remember, the purpose of New Testament prophecy is for the building up of the Church.

Clearly, no prophetic revelation would be acceptable if it contradicted established prophetic utterances already recorded in the Scriptures. For example, anyone claiming to know the day the Lord will return, no matter how they say it in the Lord's name, or how insistent they are, or what verses they use, clearly would be contradicting what the Lord Himself taught. Throughout history, there have been many such occurrences of false prophets predicting the day of the Lord's return, being wrong one-hundred percent of the time.

On the other hand, there is no way to judge someone's subjective experience, like claiming they speak to angels. I do not believe this is what Paul had in mind when he gave the instruction on judging prophecy. Paul was speaking about something that *could be* judged, verified, or confirmed by others. The prophets that you see on the internet and television, at churches and conferences are not being judged by anyone. Therefore, anything they say is accepted and goes unchallenged.

Paul's closing instruction is powerful: "If anyone thinks himself to be a prophet or spiritual, let him acknowledge that the things which I write to you are the commandments of the Lord" (1 Cor.14:37). In other words, Paul is saying this is not just some theological opinion that I am giving you; these are the commandments of the Lord. This means that when Paul instructed that prophets were to be judged, that wasn't Pauline commentary, that was a directive from the Lord Himself. Many of the prophets that you see today are allowed to get up before a congregation and say whatever they want to, with none of these pastors who invited them challenging anything they say. These pastors will give an account to the Lord for how they allowed a wolf in sheep's clothing to stand before the congregation and feed on the flock, just so big offerings could be raised.

CHAPTER 11

FINAL WORDS

It is important for those of you who have read this book to understand the purpose and gravity of the subject matter presented before you. For me this is not some soapbox that I have decided to climb upon to herald a passionately held point to sell books. No, this material seeks to address the fact that many false prophets are being sent out into the world, and to expose the acts of false prophets that the Bible warns are a sign of the "last days."

There is a wave of heretical teaching and activity that is sweeping across America. Many of these false prophets are found in churches throughout the world, but particularly in America and Africa. Many of these false prophets are reaching thousands upon thousands, with huge followings of people in every corner of the globe. Some are graduates from so-called "schools of prophets" that are cranking out prophets that have been trained in metaphysical and divination techniques that are being passed off as Bible-based and Holy Spirit-inspired ministry gifts. Though I cannot say that every school of prophets teaches divination, surely there are those that do.

Many are impressed with those who operate in forensic pinpoint prophecy, because they believe it is from God. There is great attraction to see the Spirit work. This is what happened to Simon the Sorcerer, when he beheld the miracles that Philip the Evangelist was performing. When you mix the desire to perform miracles,

> *All church leaders everywhere, regardless of denominational affiliation, must have an active apologetic as a part of their systematic study in order to protect their flocks against the damnable heresies and deception of false prophets.*

with Paul's encouragement that you all prophesy, you can end up with a seductive attraction that is hard to resist. The thrill of being the powerhouse in the room able to call out names and numbers, while people are marveling at your gift, is intoxicating. This is exactly what these con-men are looking for. They recruit students so taken in by the supernatural that they enroll in a school established by a false prophet and pay to learn these deceptive techniques.

It cannot be overemphasized how the Lord rebuked the Pharisees when He said, "A wicked and adulterous generation seeks after a sign" (Matthew 16:4, NKJV). And to His own disciples he admonished, "…do not rejoice that the spirits submit to you, but rejoice that your names are written in heaven" (Luke 10:20). This statement is critically important, because the one does not necessitate the other. In other words, just because you have authority over a demon, or the ability to prophesy, does not by itself mean that your name is written in heaven among those who have been redeemed. It is on this basis that those who teach that a person must manifest a spiritual gift as proof or validation of salvation are on a very slippery slope.

Undoubtedly, that is exactly what will happen on Judgment Day when they profess, "Lord, Lord, did we not prophesy, cast out devils, and perform miracles, in your name?" But the Lord will profess to them, "I never knew you, depart from me you workers of iniquity." It won't matter what gifts they operated in or what miracles they performed. It won't even make a difference that it was done in the Lord's name. All of this is meaningless if you are not in a relationship with Christ and your name is not written in heaven.

Like ravenous wolves, false prophets feed off of the flock, and they use divination techniques to garner favor and power amongst unsuspecting, unlearned Christians who attend their prophetic conferences and meetings, searching for a supernatural experience to satisfy their longing souls. Being fascinated by these individuals' display of so-called prophetic power, carnal Christians are taken in by superficial prognostications that are nothing more than what mediums and psychics have been doing all along. Even more dreadful are the pastors that offer up their flocks to these false prophets because of their potential to raise hefty offerings. Behind closed doors, many of these pastors know these prophets are false, but they turn a blind eye to that reality in order to raise money. Typically money, not God, is the motivating factor for these prophets to conduct revivals and conferences.

Though greedy ministers out to exploit people for their own gain have always been present, what is new is the internet. One of the false prophets used in this study has videos on YouTube with over eighty thousand views. We are in the age where ministers no longer need a church edifice to have a following. All they need is a cell phone and an internet connection, and they can reach more people than you can pack into a sports arena, all from the comfort of their living room.

As the Bible declares, many people do not want to hear sound doctrine, but instead will seek out teachers who will tickle their itching ears with foolishness and falsities. Being in the computer smartphone technology age only exacerbates this problem, because someone that no one would pay attention to in the past now has access to literally tens of thousands of people on a worldwide scale. Some of these teachers are drawing away people who attend church. While pastors seek to make the Gospel message culturally relevant to generations like the millennials, wholesome church tradition often gets left behind. To some even the word tradition has a negative connotation.

As pastors seek to become more seeker sensitive to attract a generation that is increasingly anti-establishment and anti-Church, sound doctrine can get compromised. Even the sanctuaries are becoming more like television sets with swirling graphics on jumbo screens and high-tech lights, and stages with no hint of anything sacred. The shift to an accommodation model has positioned some churches to head for shipwreck because they have slipped from traditional moorings. In a high-tech visual media age, this means there is now a shift from reverence and worship to enticement and entertainment. Therefore, false prophets are spreading, because they are mastering the media that our youth are drawn to. All of this plays right into what the Bible declares as a great falling away that will come, and is already in progress.

In this transformation, the concept of being a Christian morphs into a platform for spiritual entertainment, while the false prophets teach that a relationship with God is about receiving blessings. The way these false prophets tell it, the whole purpose of being a Christian is so God will bless you. There's no conviction of sin or a sense of reasonable service to the Lord for His name's sake. No, it's all about Me, myself, and I. Many churchgoers are not interested in righteousness or holiness, which already seems to be an archaic message. They are not interested in being born again or living according to biblical standards and ethics, but are merely seeking a spiritual, sensational experience without the guidance of truth and sound doctrine to keep them from going adrift.

Though the Bible states explicitly the reason for the five-fold ministries mentioned in Ephesians chapter 4, the whole purpose of these ministry gifts was to perfect, bring to maturity, and edify the body of Christ so that the Church's members would not fall prey to the deceptions of those waiting to deceive.

The church was never meant to become a mechanism to create super apostles, prophets, and pastors that could become famous and amass wealth. Many of these people have been called by men, and since they have been called by men, that means they have not been called or appointed by God. God calls people into the five-fold ministry. This is why the Lord emphasizes that he gave "some" Apostles, "some" prophets, "some" evangelists, and "some" pastors and teachers...." That means if you are not one of the "some," you are inevitably one of the "many" false prophets that have gone out into the world. It is these that are the false ministers, false teachers, false prophets, false apostles, and false brethren who do not operate under the power of the Lord, but operate through counterfeit charisma. It is Satan's agenda to kill, steal, and to destroy. It is Satan's agenda to transform himself into an angel of light and his ministers into ministers of righteousness. It is Satan's agenda to appear as a wolf in sheep's clothing for the explicit purpose to deceive and ultimately destroy people's souls.

Of the many signs that there are of the end times, so much emphasis is placed on the obvious signs such as wars and rumors of wars, earthquakes, weather patterns, famines, floods, and social and political unrest. We are quick to point out the advances in technology that are moving us closer to the mark of the Beast. We are amazed to see what is happening to Israel and the Middle East, but we fail to recognize another important sign of the end-times, which is the emergence of many false prophets.

Every parent, every brother and sister, every pastor, and teacher that has been called by the Lord should also be concerned that we live in the days of mass deception. Therefore, it behooves all of us who know the truth to seek the Lord in spirit and in truth. We must warn as many people as we can about the far-reaching effects of mass deception by false prophets. This is a big problem, especially amongst Pentecostal and Charismatic Christians who have an experience-based religious philosophy and belief. Due to their doctrinal position of heavy reliance on spiritual gifts as a sign of salvation, this places millions of Christians in the cross-hairs of Satan, who fosters and nourishes counterfeit gifts. Satan does not care if a person thinks they are doing Christ's work.

Another area of serious concern is the massive attack on the Word of God. New translations with political and special-interest agendas are starting to flood the markets. All of these are designed to pull people away from the truth and siphon them off from the faith. In 2 Thessalonians chapter 2, the Bible speaks of a massive falling away. Though I believe many factors contribute to this, false prophets shall lead the charge and deceive many to follow the wrong road. As Jesus said in the Gospel narratives, the road that leads to destruction is the easy road. The road with all the bright lights. The road with all the colorful neon signs. The road with all the attractions along the way. The popular road that everybody is traveling on. The road where cheap grace is found and is plentiful. The road where anyone's belief system is just as good as anyone else's. The road where conviction and discomfort do not exist. Be forewarned, there are those who are lifting Satan's banner while calling out the name of Jesus. There is nothing more horrid than that reality.

In this book I address the fact that much of this prophetic phenomenon occurs in Charismatic and Pentecostal churches. Though in general that may be the case, there are other factors that have implications for those churches and organizations outside of those parameters. Because the world is immersed in so much technology and people have access to the world through their smartphones and computers. As it has always been, pastors have no control over what their members are engaging while away from the church. Because of this, no one is out of reach of the treacherous tentacles of heresy and false prophecy. All church leaders everywhere, regardless of denominational affiliation, must have an active apologetic as a part of their systematic study in order to protect their flocks against the damnable heresies and deception of false prophets.

What I have covered in this book is only the tip of the iceberg. Time would not permit an exhaustive study on every wind of false doctrine and false prophecy. More time should be spent on people seeking the truth as revealed through Holy Scriptures. The Bible says man shall not live by bread alone, but by every word that proceedeth out of the mouth of God. Ye shall know the truth, and the truth shall make you free. See to it that no man deceives you! May the grace of our Lord Jesus Christ continue with you always, in Jesus' mighty name. Amen!

—The End

ABOUT THE AUTHOR

Dr. Dennis J. Woods has studied eschatology for over 40 years. His fascination with biblical prophecy began in 1976 after reading his first Hal Lindsey book while serving in the Navy on board the U.S.S. England. In 1982, after being honorably discharged, he continued his eschatological studies reading great dispensational teachers such as Clearance Larkin's books *Dispensational Truth, the Book of Revelation* and *Daniel*.

In 1994, Dr. Woods' first book Unlocking the Door: A Key to Biblical Prophecy was published, giving him national exposure. In 1995, he further sharpened his eschatological skills by taking a Revelation course taught by renowned New Testament theologian Dr. D.A. Carson, at *Trinity Evangelical Divinity School*, Wisconsin extension, Elm Brook Church (Dr. Steward Briscoe, Pastor). In 1997, he also corresponded with Dallas Theological Seminary pillars Dr. John Walvoord (2004) and J. Dwight Pentecost (2014).

Today, Dr. Woods is President and CEO of Life To Legacy, LLC a thriving independent book publisher having published numerous titles for various authors. He is also the pastor of Power of the Holy Ghost Deliverance Ministries, having nursing home and radio outreach ministries in Chicago IL. Dr. Woods also has the Revelation Revolution Podcast. For their spiritual enrichment he and his wife of 20 years Chantia, attend the Apostolic Church of God, of Chicago Illinois, where Dr. Byron T. Brazier is the pastor.

In 2004, Dr. Woods received his Doctorate of Biblical Studies from Midwest Theological Institute of Indiana.

All speaking engagements requests should be submitted to:

Life2legacybooks@att.net

END NOTES

INTRODUCTION

1. Hill, Jonathan, *Zondervan Handbook to the History of Christianity* (Zondervan/Lion Publishing, Grand Rapids, Mich., 2006), p. 68.
2. Ibid., p.69.

CHAPTER 1

3. Ciampa, Roy E. and Rosner, Brian S., *Pillar New Testament Commentary— The First Letter to the Corinthians* (Wm.B.Eerdmans, 2010) p. 295.

4. *James Strong's Exhaustive Concordance of the Bible*, GreekDictionary, #1985 *episkopos* (bishop).

5. Ibid., # 4245 *presbyteros* (Elder)
6. Keener, Craig, *The IVP Bible Background Commentary*—New Testament–John (IntervarsityPress,2014),p. 258.

CHAPTER 2

7. *Eusebius' Ecclesiastical History*, Book 2, Ch.13 (4) (Hendrickson Publishers, Peabody Maryland, 1998, Simon Magus.

8. *James Strong's Exhaustive Concordance of the Bible*, Greek Dictionary, #1839 *existēmi* (amazed).
9. The American Heritage Dictionary of the English Language,3rd Ed.,1992, *Sorcery.*

10. *Eusebius' Ecclesiastical History*, Book 2,Ch.13 (3) (Hendrickson Publishers, Peabody Maryland, 1998), Simon Magus.

11. *James Strong's Exhaustive Concordance of the Bible,*Greek Dictionary, #5486.

12. Easton, Matthew George,"Miracle,"*Easton's Illustrated Bible Dictionary* (1898), p. 447.

13. www.youtube.com/watch?v=krP4F1r9Vx8 (accessed1-17-18). *Voice Of An Angel - Rescuers Hear Woman Calling For Help - Fox & Friends.*

14. *The American Heritage Dictionary of the English Language* "Counterfeit"

15. Woods, Dennis James, *Counterfeit Charisma* (AmErica House, Baltimore, 2000), p. 17. *Counterfeit Charisma*

16. MacArthur, John F., *Charismatic Chaos* (Zondervan, Grand Rapids, Mich., 1992), Ch.1, p. 26.

17. Packer, J.I., *The Most Important 18 Words You Will Ever Know,* Revelation, (Christian Focus Publications, Scottland U.K., 1981) p. 27

18. Tenney, Merrill, *Zondervan Pictorial Encyclopedia of the Bible* (Zondervan, Grand Rapids, Mich.,1975), Vol.6, p. 443, Simon Magus.

19. Ibid.

20. Ibid.

21. Ibid.

22. Latourette, Kenneth, *A History of the Christian Church* (Prince Press, Peabody, Md., 1953/1975). Vol.1, p. 566. Simon Magus.

23. *The American Heritage Dictionary of the English Langauge*, Gnostic.

24. Geisler, Norman, *Baker Encyclopedia of Christian Apologetics* (Baker Books, Grand Rapids, Mich.,1992), p. 274, Gnosticism.

25. Wace, Henry, *A Dictionary of Christian Biography and Literature* Docestism.

26. Latourette, Kenneth, "Simony" *A History of Christianity*, Vol.1, Beginnings to 1500,p. 460.

27. Geisler, Norman, "Gospel of Thomas," *Baker Encyclopedia of Christian Apologetics* (Baker Books, Grand Rapids, Mich., 1992), p. 297.

28. Smith's Bible Dictionary: Comprising Antiquities, Biography, Geography, Natural History, Archaeology and Literature,"Simon Magus."

Chapter 3

29. *Strong's Greek Dictionary*,4183. *polys* (many).

30. Baldwin, Joyce G.,*Tyndale Old Testament Commentaries*–1and 2 Samuel(Intervarsity Press,1988), p.124.
31. Green, Michael, *Tyndale New Testament Commentaries*–2Peter and Jude (Intervarsity Press,1987), p.116.
32. Peterson, David G., *Pillar New Testament Commentary*–TheActs of the Apostles (Eerdmans, Grand Rapids, Mich.,2009) p. 574.

33. Zodhiates, Spiro *The Complete Word Study Dictionary*, New Testament *Rhema* #4487 prediction, prophecy III (B).

Chapter 4

34. Tenney, Merril, *Zondervan Pictorial Encyclopedia of the Bible*, Angel of the Lord (Zondervan, Grand Rapids, Mi., 1975) Vol. 1, pg 163.

Chapter 5

35. Ibid.,Vol.2, p. 146 Divination.

36. *Smith's Bible Dictionary*: Divination Comprising Antiquities, Biography, Geography, Natural History, Archaeology and Literature.

37. Struthers, Jane, " FaceReading," *The Fortune-Tellers'Bible:A Definitive Guide to the Arts of Divination* (SterlingPublishing,N.Y./London, 2007), p. 304.
38. Ibid., "Numerology," p. 100.

39. Ibid.,p.100.

40. Ibid., "Numerology,"p. 103.

41. Tenney, Merrill, *Zondervan Pictorial Encyclopedia of the Bible* (Zondervan, Grand Rapids, Mich.,1975),Vol. 2, p. 146, Chresmology.

42. Ibid., "Oneiromancy," p.146-147.

43. Ibid., "Astrology" p.147.

44. Ibid.,"Necromancy" p.147.

45. https://www.youtube.com/watch?v=V252j868jTk (Marjoe accessed1-8-18).

CHAPTER 6

46. http://www.psychicreviewonline.com/?t202id=1997&t202kw=psychic%20friends, (accessed1-1-18).

47. http://www.fengshuifortunetelling.com/fortune-telling-1.html.

CHAPTER 7

48. *Encyclopedia of Religious Phenomena*, "Psychic and Paranormal," p. 115. Visible Ink Press (September 1, 2007).

49. Ibid., "Mediums and Mediumship," p. 220.

50. Ibid.

51. *New World Dictionary of the American Language*, Second College Ed. *Metaphysical.*

52. http://www.wholesomeayurveda.com/2017/07/07/om-aum-meditation-science-benefits/

53. http://altered-states.net/barry/newsletter463/(accessed12/15/17).

54. Lea,Thomas D., "Jannes and Jambres,"*New American Commentary*, Vol.34:1, 2 Timothy, Titus (B&H Publishing Group, 1992), p. 227.

55. Enns, Peter, "Jannes and Jambres," *The NIV Application Commentary*–Exodus, (Zondervan, Grand Rapids, Mich.,2000), p. 183.

56. Ibid., p. 208.

57. http://remoteviewed.com/remote_viewing_history_military.htm (accessed 7-1-18).

CHAPTER 8

58. *Strong's Hebrew Dictionary*, 4886: "to rub with oil, i.e. to anoint; by implication to consecrate."
59. Ibid., 5480: to smear over (with oil).

60. *Strong's Greek Dictionary*, 218: to oil (with perfume).

61. Ibid., 3462: to apply (perfumed) unguent.

62. Ibid., 2025: to smear over.

63. Ibid., 5548: to consecrate to an office or religious service.

64. Ibid., 5547: anointed, i.e., the Messiah, an epithet of Jesus.

65. *Strong's Hebrew Dictionary*, 4899: a consecrated person (as a king, priest, or saint); specifically, the Messiah, anointed, Messiah.

66. *Strong's Greek Dictionary*, 5545: the special endowment ("chrism") of the Holy Spirit, anointing, unction.

67. Tenney, Merril, *Zondervan Pictorial Encyclopedia of the Bible*, (Zondervan, Grand Rapids, Mi., 1975) Vol.5, pg 832, "Tyre".

68. Cooper Sr., Lamar E.,"Ethbaal II," *New American Commentary*, Vol.17: Ezekiel (B&H Publishing Group, 1994), p. 260.

69. Davids, Peter H., "Assumption of Moses," *Pillar New Testament Commen tary*—Commentary on Jude (Eerdmans Publishing,2006), p. 59.

70. *Strong's Greek Dictionary*, anti-christ #500: an *opponent of the Messi ah*-antichrist.

CHAPTER 9

71. Boice, James Montgomery, "Love not the World," *Boice Expositional Commentary* The Epistles of John (Baker Book House,1979), p. 62.

72. Cole, Alan R., *Tyndale New Testament Commentaries*—Galatians (Inter-varsity Press,1989), p. 213.

73. Boice, James Montgomery Genesis, *Boice Expositional Commentary* Vol.2: A New Beginning, p. 520.

74. https://youtu.be/CMrFCwYAZxE, Jonestown Suicide Tape.

75. Davids, Peter H., *Pillar New Testament Commentary*- Commentary on Jude, (Eerdmans Publishing, 2006) pg 219.

76. Ibid.

77. Matthew George Easton, *Easton's Illustrated Bible Dictionary* (1898), pg. 578, Prophet.

78. Strongs, Hebrew Dictionary, 4932, Mishneh.

79. Tenney, Merril, *Zondervan Pictorial Encyclopedia of the Bible*, (Zondervan, Grand Rapids, Mi., 1975) Prophets and Prophecy, pg 884.

80. Wiseman, Donald, J., Tyndale Old Testament Commentaries 1 and 2 Kings, Vol. 9 – pg 317, Mishneh.

81. Tenney, Merril, *Zondervan Pictorial Encyclopedia of the Bible*,

(Zondervan, Grand Rapids, Mi., 1975), Prophets and Prophecy, pg 884.

CHAPTER 10

82. Morris, Leon *The Pillar New Testament Commentary* (Intervarsity Press 1984), – The Letters to the Thessalonians, pg 260.

83. Wuest, Kenneth, *The New Testament, An Expanded Translation,* Vol.2, Wm B. Eerdmans Publishing Company, 1973, pg 483.

84. Bruce, F.F., *Word Bible Commentary*, First Letter to the Thessalonians, On Various Christian Duties, p. 125.

85. Strong's Greek Dictionary, #3619 (edifying) a structure; figurative confirmation, building, "edify".

86. Strong's Greek Dictionary, #1252 *judgment.*

ABOUT THE PUBLISHER

Let us bring your story to life! With Life to Legacy, we offer the following publishing services: manuscript development, editing, transcription services, ghostwriting, cover design, copyright services, ISBN assignment, worldwide distribution, and eBook production and distribution.

Throughout the entire production process, you maintain control over your project. We also specialize in family history books, so you can leave a written legacy for your children, grandchildren, and others. You put your story in our hands, and we'll bring it to literary life! We have several publishing packages to meet all your publishing needs.

Call us at: 877-267-7477, or you can also send e-mail to: Life2Legacybooks@att.net. Please visit our Web site:

www.Life2Legacy.com